CONTENTS

WE HAVE EACH OTHER IN THE FAMILY

An intertwined true life happenings...
If only you were there to

HELP!

**"The only difference between Paradise and Hell
Is the preference of the self-deceiver?
The Future has nothing better to offer
Than further suffering and achievement.
The desire to avoid suffering is the longing to be dead.
In death there is no rest.
The atoms cannot surrender to silence."**

*wing wah, seow kin, yanghan,
joddi*

ACKNOWLEDGEMENT:

My Family and I are thankful to Amazon Kindle Direct Publishing for providing a cost-efficient publishing platform to enable author of all walk of life to reach every corner of the world with their "dream book" into reality or it still remains a dream.

We must thank most humbly to your purchase because you have given this book "WE HAVE EACH OTHER IN THE FAMILY...an intertwined true life happenings... if only you were there to help" a chance to breathe life in it in a big way. Where there is life there is hope. Hope gives Life.

Life is a single aspect of our existence so do Living is more remarkable than Life. Without which Life cannot remarked upon. This book will not end our acquaintance because there is angling thought the "Counting steps to your heart" are left with that which is subtle is never ending only beginning...

GENTLE PRAYER;

…Believe me it is not easy to write about our plight and predicament
accompanied pains and sufferings, agony and torment for
my family and I are being the fallen
victim and victimized time and again.
Let alone the impact that has inflicted
Upon my family and the loved ones
And needless to say
HELP!
is not coming our way.
We got to have patience and time is running out on us
Because of our ill health cum old age.
Time indeed is cruel
when we have not much to spare.
Words
cannot express exactly as to how we feel
But we tried to match
that moment as it happened…
HELP!
will come because that is only hope we hope for
*As long as we will not give up **HOPE***
HELP!
*will come in **God**speed*

"May Each Day Find You Awakening
To A Deeper Realization of Divine Presence
Within And Around YOU"

-Divine Mama in heaven 1990s

HOME THAT WE BELONG OF YESTERYEAR...

"The First Stone Ever Chipped By Design Was The Foundation Stone Of The First City. The City Is The Cancer That Gives Life. The Ancients Mixed Their Mortar With Blood. With Blood It Endures. Blood Is The Mortar Of All Cities. Individuals Are Born And Die. The City Lives. Blood Is The Mortar Of All Cities. The First Permanent Feature Of The City Was The Graveyard. No City Can Be Completely Obliterated: The Remains Forever A Model Of Suffering And Achievement."

-yonder years, mum.

At Block 7 Unit #01-94 TIONG BAHRU /Singapore where I was born 04/02/1955 that made me rightfully a TAN-JONG PAGAR constituent. I am a Singapore born Chinese, now age 64s, I am considered myself an old weed. The more I am cut down, the more I spring up again. Wisdom usually grows up on us like calluses when we are old, gnarled and bent. I go where the wind blows me. I am chronically ill sick man for almost half of my life span with a diseased body that has no chance of gainfully employed. I am an undischarged bankrupt due to prolong unemployment and ill health since 2002s. I am an ex-offender for shop theft in 2011s. I am no stealer still that made me an unlikely person who someone would come to offer uncommon help. I am an outcast and condemned. It is societal stigma that inherited from Stone Age to Modern Man. I made mistake and paid for a price dearly. This is a ruthless world and one must be ruthless to cope with it.

There are more melancholy problems that confronted me and it would not go away anytime. I stood up for my family for they are my life. I am willing to put my life on the line for my family. What we have now is what we have each other in the family that gives me and us the strength to face our ongoing plight and predicament.

We find divine solace in within. Deep down we all have a sense of our own inadequacy about coping with life. It is something that all of us hide from the world yet it feeds the soul and endows our personality with charm. Most all our worldly troubles are only drifting bubbles. Most all our cares and sorrows are gone with our tomorrows.

I find comforting words to whisper to my loved ones yet I am the one who needed it most "So don't you let them fret you or someday they will get you. When skies are grey, stop work and play, and laugh your cares away"... No I want the other side of the coin, a simpler personal sense of living - not the ostentatious avenues and towering buildings which are an ever-reminder of big business and its ponderous achievements. To live in order to reason or to reason in order to live; there are the questions unanswered. It's more than the cold, hunger and the shame of poverty are more likely to affect my psychology. The world has given me its best and little of its worst. Whatever were my ill vicissitudes, I believe that fortune and ill-fortune drift upon one haphazardly as clouds. Knowing this, I am never too shocked at the bad things that happen and am agreeably surprised at the good.

I have no design for living, no philosophy - whether sage or fool, I must struggle with life. I vacillate with inconsistencies; at times small things will annoy me and catastrophes will leave me indifferent. Pessimistic but still there is hope, for I have that priceless quality of being curious about life and things which keeps up my enthusiasm. Time heals, and experience teaches that the secret of happiness is in service to other.

As I grow older I am becoming more preoccupied with faith. We live by it more than we think and achieve by it more than we realize. I believe that faith is a precursor of all our ideas. Without faith, there never could have evolved hypothesis, theory, science or mathematics. I believe that faith is an extension of the mind. It is the key that negates the impossible. To deny faith is to refute oneself and the spirit that generates all our creative forces. There must also be a fervent love of and belief in oneself. Like everyone else I am what I am: an individual, unique and different, with a lineal history of ancestral promptings and urgings; a history of dreams, desires, and of special experiences, all of which I am the sum total.

By sheer perseverance to the point of madness. One must have a capacity to suffer anguish and sustain enthusiasm over a long period of time. Perhaps it is easier for some people than others, but I doubt it. If we hold this thought, work with this thought, live with this thought, it will generate a spirit that will increase our energy and quicken our drive.

Let us strive for the impossible. Remember the great achievements throughout history have been the conquest of what seemed the impossible. My happiest days are those in which I do good work; Changi airport terminal one thru' three where display a sophistication lines of state of art automation only can be seen at the rear in the highly restricted areas not accessible to the public. Where the spirit does not work with the hand there is no art.

Mr Lee Kuan Yew (1st Singapore Prime Minister) / LKY indeed was all too awe of our local design & built creation. Port of Singapore Authority / PSA incorporated the world leading locally created high technological electronic seal for containers making clearance fastest ever in the region thus went on in acquiring multi million dollars consortium participation projects with Europe and US. Incorporating German technological power transmission

in Refuse Handling Equipment for

Housing Development Board public housing and bottling industries with new advent technological know-how has made them amongst the world best; namely Tiger breweries, Fraser and Neave, Yeo Hiap Seng, Gardenia Bread and many more. It is partaking experience like a matrix-formation of rearrangement of archaic atom from one project to another is the source of self-renewal strive. The Mind wants more.

The deeper the truth in a creative work, the longer it will live. Machinery should be a blessing to mankind and not a curse. Therefore, let us have shorter hours of labour and cheaper money. The purchasing power comes through wages. Then let us raise them to where each man can enjoy the blessings and the glory of science, which were not created for profit alone, but to serve humanity also.

A TIME BOMB WITHOUT ARMS...

A man is what a woman makes him and a woman makes herself. Both my wife, 60s and I, 64s were born in the 50s. Most of grandparent and parent have had painful experience of World War II. The aftermath of each domains bring sufferings. There were diseases and hunger everywhere. I hope we shall abolish all the hydrogen and atom bombs before they abolish us first. Not long after the World War II which countless innocent lives were lost. Then we witnessed the Korean wars that span from 50s to

53s involving US, USSR, North and South Korea plus communist China. Millions of innocent lives too were killed. North and South Korea were separated and most painful moment was to see the breaking up of a happy home. Many or thousand families were separated for a price they paid for wars. Mid 60s, the communist China successfully developed nuclear bombs and its allies North Korea also succeeding nuclear capability. It is not a good sign for the World and to its immediate neighbouring countries. Life would not be the same if there are such outbreak. It would not be conventional wars. The magnitude of destruction of nuclear and chemical warfare are beyond our apprehension because it is too huge. The wounded Earth could not heal itself quicker and life on Earth would not be the same. It cannot regenerate and sustain the eco-lives. Earth cannot produce enough oxygen anymore for the world to breathe. Man and any living beings will die by days even the babies cannot survive and born deformed. Sun draws the Earth closer because the Earth has served its purposes and of no use to the Universe. Earth will become a gigantic burning mass inside the Sun to fuel a new born planet to come to being. **Universe is outside Time.** Earth is not far off to end its existence just a button away. Why? When Earth's life is only left 80 billion light years:

"Time exists within the Universe. The Universe is outside Time. Therefore the Universe is without Future. The Universe moves from Infinity towards Unity. Time is the reduction of the numbers of Infinity towards Unity. Time ravels the particles of which it is an expression. Man is a tool created by the Universe in order to mark Time. Time is the expression of infinite and discrete points of energy reducing their numbers in the search for Unity, thus progressively reducing the infinitude of their own mathematical possibilities. Universe means "movement towards ONE"

"The desire for peace is universal. I do not assume to know the answers to the problems which threaten peace, but this I do know: that nations will never solve them in an atmosphere of hate or suspicion; nor will the threat of dropping hydrogen bombs solve them. The melancholy grooming of people to the acceptance of hydrogen warfare, with all its attendant horrors, is a crime against the human spirit and has created world infirmity. Let us therefore absolve ourselves of the miserable, cancerous atmosphere. Let us try to understand each other's problems, for in modern warfare there is no victory."

In 2018s, Singapore even though small in size took the initiative

to partake to hold to the 1st ever round table talk between the two leaders US President Donald Trump and North Korea Mr Kim Jong Un towards denuclearization of North Korea. Singapore will go down in history to be an avenue to such important event. History was made just as LKY's (truly a honourable man, *Mr Lee Kuan Yew*) address to the US congressmen for an ordinary Asian size shoes were too small for the American but he made an imprint altogether to bridge two huge markets with great potential and bring about business spinoffs by opening up its doors to trades. The economic transformation see the increase of millionaires to billionaires in US and so do China. Once the barefooted China is now on wheel with full throttle in opening up its doors to the

world. China gone on to become 2nd economic superpower. It is not miracle but of sure grit of I.5 billion people making it a real miracle. We can never find another LKY. His unique voice with depth of conviction as he speaks without texts made him a natural born leader. He is fearless to cross straits to where the unlikely places that infested with fanatic who find him pain in the neck. His gesticulated style with words were classic. Too giggle and tickle the funny bones "when you've the urge, go and chew a banana." Beethoven would die laughing because of his symphony no 5 of well-hidden favourite musical quote cum melody was a *ba..na..na*. His simple testament is truth to live and let live, be it near or far. A man's tear is not his weakness but having being strong far too long. It is not coming from the brain but purely from his heart. He is what he is. I am awe to this Man. I am glad and honour to witness such a great leader in my lifetime. We have nothing in any common lineage but just a citizen and a leader that lie the tie. Mama always said good leaders or government built roads, houses and enough food to eat. Mama did not live long to see it but I am sure and heaven is fair that she will get her chance when she reborn. Mama and LKY had something in common to what I feel in astral senses within that inexpressible in words. Mama was dying on Friday 29/12/1990 and LKY was admitted to SGH hospital for critical condition on one of the Saturday before the weeks of Chinese New Year 2015. The feeling which I got was the same on 29/12/1990s. It made me feel not right like my inner compass had stopped, I cannot move but circling aimlessly. Maybe the tie we have is strong only limited to divine explanation. I will remember on the very day of sending off the weather was deep in solemn. Heaven was opening up with heavy downpour in a while was a prelude to receive a good soul and well-orchestrated cool breeze then subtle rain become migrating mist come and go that lasted till dawn. It was a divine blessing to witness and be part of that passing movement. I stood still and let it fall on my face in a way to acknowledge. I always like walking in the rain and that the only way I can hide my crying. Asian are hardworking people. They put hard work for the sake of their families even their lives on the line for the country. Five thousand years of history is not just a culture but real ingrain coming to fold towards arriving a unit with great mathematical possibilities. They want their children to have better life and good future. Singapore has its fair share of economic successes all for a balance trades with its global players. We know we cannot take success for granted. We are mindful not to be complacent too. We are taught by our forefathers that the position we occupy is not so important than the direction we are moving in. LKY shows us that we can be "monstrous" in our attempt not be conditioned by a mere size in moving forward. "Ant can leap to become a mammoth!" We are with him in all good ways. Papa taught us our siblings thru him of what he had gone thru the earlier years, of shape of things in the 60s. There were upheaval of the pro-Communists to destabilize the country, secret societies to fight for territorial controls, street gangster aimless wasted bloodsheds, mobbed fighting for delinquent pastimes, racial riots are all too colour blind, and demonstrations was the only way to park buses on the double yellow and throw away the keys, the big BUKIT HO SWEE fire burned whatever come its ways to the ground and see the aftermath ruin was a wasted quilt coupled with economic hardships on living edge but happy to have each other in the family. Such baptism of fire awaken to a hero of that era.

His and that is LKY's indomitable grit and legacy will live on forever in our hearts and to the future generation to come. He gave us something to hate about and appreciate it in later years. I myself hate military services, a rocker of the hyped of hippies' cultures of 70s but there again we were young then and to stay away from the street life was for everyone good thus good for the country. LKY pitched "broken necks and bones" once in a while to remind us the terror of the 60s.

He may not be around but we are always here for Singapore. It is the only way to be a grown up man just for him and for the country, who done so much in one lifetime. There is no science to it to understand why? We were born here! We die here! We are old now and we want to die a happy death less mundane shortcomings.

TIONG BAHRU WHERE WE LOVE WHEN WE PLAY...

How we see poverty and bitter privation, with a longing which knows it can never be satisfied but **TIONG BAHRU** will always filled with a place where there are the scene of frolic, gaiety and extravagant adventure. We were young and care free. *We love when we play*. We know we have to be home at dawn. We will start all over again with same gusto and vehemence the next day. We were barefooted and running wild chasing wind.

Our parent understood freedom and let their young have it without putting a fight. They were once been deprived due to wars. Our parent are conservative and protective, they still carried out tradition practises especially come to family lineage the boy stands to have more privilege than girl. The girl will somehow deprived of going to school. If the family is not well to do then girls are either end up helping their mother in household chores or working in the nearby shop as an odd job helper doing strenuous work with long hours or in a factory as an operator spend 8hrs or more looking at the magnified glass in assembly works.

My wife could have make it further in her pursuit in study but dropped out of secondary school. Her family could not cope with the rising costs. Her parents were fruits seller, doing what they could to feed the family of 6 children and barely make ends meet. Her father passed away at early age and for a reason she has to work to supplement her family incomes.

My wife was only 15yrs old and started as a factory operator. She has to spend 10hrs every day in looking thru the magnifying glass to sort out tiny little electronic parts. She made time to help out in her parents' fruit makeshift stall. Her mother was overly protective as she was the youngest daughter and also showered most of maternal love among the siblings nonetheless being berated at slight instance. Parent are good at not to show love openly yet they prejudiced their own action.

Those were the days where many families live in such economic conditions but we are still the happy lots because **we have each other in the family**. We are lucky not to starve quietly. Neighbours were warmth and helpful. We see few bucks exchanging hands in time of need. Vegetables, rice, soy sauce, chilli, egg and other convenient things went around just to make way to whom in need. We would not miss a feast if any neighbour had a celebration. A celebrated neighbour would dropped by with food to grace the occasion. Relatives and friends cramped up the dining hall like sardines to feast. Noisy environment but lively, shouting, talking and calling from every corners echoing thru the nights. The black and white TV console (old folk describe it as look like chicken backside) was the first introduction to a new era and together with radio jukebox (as the old think "evil talker") had changed the way we live.

Then arrival of sound blaster system with loudspeakers was to drive the neighbour nut and mama had to scream to make her presence felt "are you trying to wake up the dead." So even in death atom cannot succumb to silence. We missed the yore of

time and precious moments. Time is cruel. It leaves the past abruptly to catch up the future faster than we think. Those moments were precious indeed. Man was made to make things and so do man was created to protect woman. I was blessed to have a good loving mother. She taught us thru love. From her love I realize strength in within.

It gives me courage to face the outside world. The world that freedom within that I hope for under a big starry sky for all to share. One lifetime, one sky to share.

WHERE THERE IS WORK THERE IS A FUTURE...

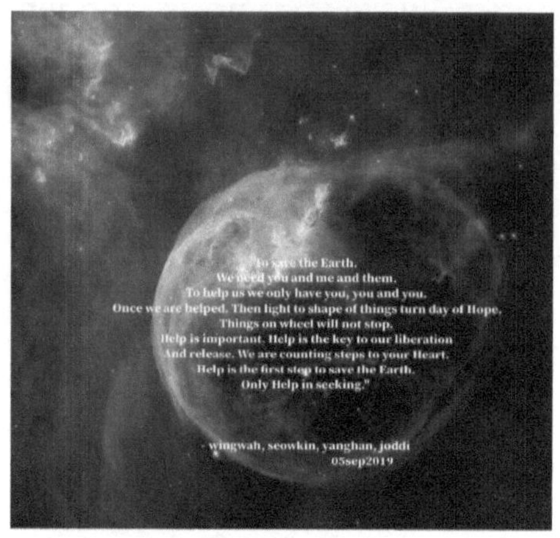

At mid age for a young man to take up two jobs in a day was telling I was loaded with energy. I worked as a Service Technician in the day into office automation work and night shift as a permanent 2nd Shift Production Supervisor at INCOM International specializing in manufacturing and assembly of ACME roller chains. Most of female production operators were of matured age.

They made it hard to take order from me because they thought I was just another young and inexperienced college boy. I proved them wrong in overtime and patience. I won them over, bind and train them into champion production team. They always overtaken the production target and left 1st shift run out of production work. I got slammed from the production manager of overdoing or overstepping the boundary.

It is good to know appreciation and recognition were seem to be no middle ground. It signalled to me the time to move. Majority of 2nd shift production team were sadden and cried. My heart jerked in awaken to separation of closed togetherness and they really taken me in as their familial son. Barely 2 years with them what if 10 years! I cannot imagine. What I taught them was what my mama did thru love. I could feel the feeling love when I with them. There was enough love to go around then. They do not expect me to know but to understand.

Those operators who were expecting would enjoy much freedom

than others. Elderly of course shared the same attention. I provided them security when they are with me. I do not speak Malay but someone from the leader of the pack will interpret. I told them as long as there is upmost trust. There would not be a wall between us. Then harmony working together is natural thing.

I punched the air "Merdeka!" they all looked strange but when I shouted "go home lah.." when job is done they all flied like bullets.

Only LKY synced the chord in perfection,

"Merdeka!!!"

*"When we reach for a new height
we must continue to strive
one inch at time
to make a mile of difference"*

MY SOUL MATE COURTING GIFTS PLUS ADULT TOYS...

I met my wife in a most peculiar way. "So close yet so far" is a familiar phrase. In 1986s, I have had a shop in Tanglin Shopping Centre at third floor with registered company named TOPOGRAPHIC Pte Ltd specialize in selling US-Japanese made sublimation imprint machines. We have secured the distribution right for Far East markets but we loss the distribution right a year later to TRANMARCO Group hence our business partnership ended prematurely. I was a shareholder with equal share in the company. The two other business partners were into distribution of reputed European automobiles and ship chandlers business. I carry on the retail business. With technical knowhow I managed to modify & improve the machine versatility in term of its function capability. It can be interchangeable as a conventional copier and sublimation imprint machine. The retail imprint services business was good and sustainable to earn enough to pay the landlord monthly rental but unable to cope with the ever lease rental increase. I wanted to take the business to next level and I needed fund to realize my plan. I have good gadgetry in my pocket for commercial usages and awarded government (SISSIR)/SITAS grant limiting to fabrication and prototype making. In 1990s I foresee more on-line businesses so I try to tap into the Web Wide World engines to start up on-line business with huge market potential but only met with disappointment, all because of our local banks were not ready to establish merchant account for online order processing.

I only met my wife by chance. All this while she was on 1st floor boutique shop and I was on 3rd floor. We met at the cafeteria. It was lunch time and crowded. We only able to make some silent psychic and mimic contact "are you with me" and silly movement just to catch each other eyes. A lightning bolt is all we need and moment is just about right, there and then we felt strongly for each other. Something of a "pull and push" (PAP) of a hearty feeling that inexpressible in words which got us into a world within a world. Both our search ended and a new life begin, having each other arms together is a wonderful comforting feeling and to have little kiddo on the way a year later when we got married was a pledge of our love. We do have ups and downs. At times our relationship gone into binaries of fire and water showdowns. Its essence we see to build our relationship stronger later on but never water and oil for we know it brings destructive and endless harms to the family and kin. Of course we have standoff and impasse that last for few days. The in-laws were domineering and headstrong at first towards our relationship. Much to my persistent angling of "push and pull" (PAP) techniques to charm cum patience in wait only then my mother in-law acknowledge in acceptance to have me as part of her family. I was into good mix of east and west cultures but she want more of the east in me.

I finally decided to give up the retail business and take up a full time job. From business development to manufacturing, design and build to sales and marketing. I have learned to garner such knowledge and use it most readily for future challenges. I went on to join other companies with specialization fields to gain more knowledge so to scale upward. SEW EURODRIVE was the next stop. A German assembly plant in TUAS/JURONG industry specializes in assembly of power transmission, geared motors, and gear boxes and so on. Normally I would do a brief summary check of the company which I shortlisted for interview. I was asking myself as to how on earth I got a wink of sewerage experience.

Too late for piecing with no ends. I went for the interview and surprised by interviewer was not a German origin as the company impressed upon but a soft spoken tanned skin Asian man who will be my immediate boss, Mr Baek. I also met Ms Florence Kok the company secretary. Her hairdo impressed me till now was out of cult. I can never find another hair stylist who patiently spurn her every strand of hair into curly precision. Her perfume she carried was good enough to smother a platoon of flies if not swamp. A lasting impression went both ways. Here they got their man who does a job right at first time and done the company proud. I got great memories to lean back and reminiscing. Good for the company but bad disposition for me: I recaptured project orders back alive when business deals were already closed or awarded to other competitor. I infiltrated competitor stronghold to audit the stock position to gather its strength and weakness to compete to our advantage. Achieving the best project sales overall was not my upmost goal but knowing my true worth to go beyond my limitation is worthy of gold and creating self-challenge is by far my inward passion. Hearty good moments to cherish. Wedding bells blue, arrival of new born baby, passing of my beloved mama, driving a new BMW with VANOS engine which I longed and bringing better comfort stay with full facilities home for my family all these a bitter sweet happenings while I as with SEW EURODRIVE. I could have make it far better if I stay a little longer but as it seem there were working colleagues are prying their craft to assassinate my job. Worse off the main man was in water and oil contention that we cannot see eye to eye. I am sad to leave but happy to welcome a new challenge that in store for me to partake and start all over again with same violent rectitude and gusto. I had opportunity to work in a small scale Austrian assembly plant set-up also into power transmission but of lower end range capability to cater for light industries usages. I was ambitious to acquire big scale projects to compete with the market

players in power transmission. I managed to capture the 1st phase of projects order to supply 500 sets of the specific power transmission to be incorporated in the refuse handling equipment and thereafter option of 500 sets. I was too happy but short-lived because the local director was not in favour due to marginal profit. The Austrian owner wanted a higher profit margin and he had the last say. It was difficult to move into the market with no support from the top. I do not like night entertainment nor dark shabby places where the Austrian boss interested. It was always against my principle and conscience to go against moral planes. They terminated my employment and withhold my 2 months' salary all because the creditors or customers did not make payment. I was scouted and invited to join a local plastic injection moulding plant to spearhead the business development unit.

The local Chinese boss was good and happy about my business plan but muted because the local boss procrastinated so the new business was shelved. The touch screen was the in thing then and eco-friendly pallet were growing market demand thus brought about introduction to the company a new manufacturing and production capability with synergistically collaboration from the higher learning institutions and government sectors.

What I come to know with different company set ups the main man behind the local businesses had the fear of sabotages where else the other foreign business entity anticipate enjoyment come before hard work to the extent flirting with office female staff. I'm sick to all these moral principle negativity.

MAN WITH DEEP THOUGHT HAD
LITTLE CONVERSATION...

My wife 27s, was a full time homemaker then and my only son barely 5s.I was 31s making my career felt in specialized robotic, power transmission and automation engineering. I spearhead the Business Development and Marketing department of Messrs Yoshida Seiki Corp. I was moulded to be all-rounder from administration, project procurement, design and build, to manufacturing plus project commissioning and acquiring licence work head thru BCA/SISSIR (MND BLDG) so to participate $10 mil above projects. I mustered the advent of technological transfers over the period of 15 years, learning the specialized trade from the German, American & Japanese from synergy or consortium projects thereby the business spinoff benefited wide spectrum of diverse industries locally - airports, seaports, manufacturing etc., Japanese have their very own working culture. Japanese is uniquely that stand out in work ethnic coupled with 1st class comradeships. The financial crisis 1998s had bring out the true Japanese in them. Each of the Japanese managers without qualms withdrew monies from their very own personal bank account to defray the workers' wages and the chairman himself sold his property in Japan with the proceed to pay the shortfall. I was moved to tear and so do my local departmental staff! It happened right before me and it's very real. When come to facing crisis they moved as one! They do not look upon who you are but what you are so their make-up is tough as steel.

Luckily we are blessed to have LKY (1st Prime Minister – *Mr Lee Kuan Yew*) who makes Singapore "The World becomes the World to The World becomes a World" that we call HOME. This is a man left us with his legacy (2015s) and all he wants us is to build on it. Building a nation never stop because future do not allow. Once it stops there is no more future and it is simple as that. Great achievement bring great changes so do changes. Changes need great sacrifices.

I believe my generation had learn a lot from LKY's era. "To be the best of what you can" is what stand out. Many of my associates are good at innovation; a device to install in a car to enable the engine to maximize complete combustion hence minimise unburnt exhaust fume and redirect to complete the full combustion cycle. Electronic seal for cargo container handling management, Solar power energy only limited by imagination of its wide and diverse application for aging population aided apparatus need. So do I also into environmental equipment and commercial gadgetry with potential end users to name a few.
My generation are such breed are the best of macro-economists to bridge precious knowledge abound to the promising young and next generation with aged old wisdoms.

ASIAN FINANCIAL CRISIS 1998S...
WE WERE CRUSHED!

The financial crisis 1998s made its presence felt but slowly. Whoever worked in Japanese MNC companies were axed then aftermath exodus set on wheels, all because of relocation plan. Shape of things were indeed worrisome. About 300s head counts to stay to labour on without pay. Any sizable projects acquired were to sustain company business. I was retrenched with my own accord so the based workers can battle on, still I went back to do what it needs to be done to help to complete end to end projects, The chairman Mr Yoshida San was thankful but never minced a word. I went for job interviews and many job employment attempts - any job will do but same comment "over qualified or too old for the job" even I come up with "hire me only endeavour" – a drafting business proposal for potential employer to evaluate instead been exploited I put myself up for auction to the extent "pay me only if target is met". I ended up washing dishes at vegetarian store "Ru Yi" at Bukit Merah Central for $25/day but skin allergy stopped me. I waste no time and set up **Young Inventor Club** for Anderson Primary School (Principal/Mr Lawrence Leong) where my son was schooling. I wanted to provide a bridge for the student to understand and know greater insight of things about robotic engineering and automation that they are old enough one day to embrace its advent. To instil innovation and creativity when young. Organize Plant tours and Seminar cum talk by reputed field specialists and visiting consultant. Attract other schools of same approach collectively then globally making Singapore's one dot of uniquely innovation hub for the young with future extension to **Asperger** with specialized skill. This in turn attract foreign talent to come with their young to our shore to make good their next homestay. But halfway meeting with my creditor for restructuring of repayment proposal plan I collapsed because of heart attack. NTUC Insurance rejected my claim on technicality ground. The income insurance agent Lionel lee went missing when we need him most. I was totally disappointed, weak and confined in bed even though struggling, to put up several appeal attempts went vertical to CEO Mr Tan KL and ex-PM Goh but failed. I was heavily insured with NTUC to protect my family. My coverage totally to $1 million yet I get nothing in return when I landed in hospitals almost died. Technicality was a cruel word to use when my family and I were badly in need of help. Without help my family and I, our lives spiralled down quicker than a wounded falcon to the ground. The insurance agent still going around selling his stuffs like nobody business. Not even a single get well card or hospital visit for he is too guilty and ashamed to stand before me. I spent almost $2k to service the monthly NTUC insurance premiums. He would come to my house uninvited and talked about how tough he had to support his family only in wanting me to suck up another insurance policy.

Bad people brings bad experience I am lost, hopeless and despair but I fight on for the sake of my family.

ADJUDGED BANKRUPT A LIVING HELL 2002S... XXXHEART ATTACKS

2002s - Both my wife and I were made adjudged bankrupt at 47s due to ill health and prolong unemployment. My wife was due to joint liability for housing loan. It was a year after my mother in-law passed away. My wife was very sad and kept solemn to herself. Insolvency had me finally after all the trying, proposal settlement one after another rejected and repayment restructuring attempts failed. Everything literally all gone! My wife 43s and son 14s plus my therapy dog Joddi were all left homeless. Without roof over our heads let alone a fixed abode. No MPs can take up my case because I do not have a fixed abode to detail our residency so to make good of representation so no case file so territorial rule come first. I was like running up the hill most of time in seeking help and face rejections many times over. It was tedious & taxing to move temporary lodging one after another. I have to put up a strong front so not to let my family too worry. I cannot rest my tired bones and my mind was all wrecked up to deal with important issues on all fronts, finding temporary lodging in close proximity as possible to my son school then location just about good to take public transport in convenience for both my son and wife. Most importantly a timely livelihood to sustain the family economic need or defray medical expenses and so on. I have a good friend Roy Ng whom I known during Military Service. He would help me out $100 in good day just to get me going. I was too cramped up in my mind. I realised I am just a little man to face so many daunting tasks and going at me in one big wave. My body taken the toll and gone uprising. It wrecks the spot where it most life threatening that is my heart. It started from a dizzy spell and body felt numb. The accompanied gastric pain was unbearable then I collapsed on the floor. I can hear my heart shout "stop it I cannot take it anymore" next thing I know I was in hospital bed. In the midst of heart attack while I was in the daze there were noises and voices echo in my head "you cannot leave us now, our son is still young". There were battles going on inside me, I was fighting and struggling to stay alive. I was bargaining with my maker to let me live and promised to make good of the borrowed time to help whatever I can for the needy and the poor, A pendulum was swinging back and forth inside my head and add to it my head was in the top spin not to mention pounding heavily like it was going to split into halves. My blood pressure went up to 200+ mark as I was told by the staff nurse. I was hospitalised for heart attack at Mount ALVERNIA hospital. I undergone MRA scan, nucleus dye injection to my heart, treat mill tests, the X-ray scan shown my heart with abnormal size then just few weeks later I have another heart attacks that landed me at TAN TOCK SENG Hospital. This time around before I got admitted the front desk staff asked for $600 deposit prior to admission but I have only 50 bucks in my pocket. I have to tell them with one dying eye that I am having a heart attack. They deliberate while my heart take a time-out before continue my heart attacking – what a joke! So to them $600 is worthy a heart attack without which is not worth a try. The visiting heart surgeon from Mount Elisabeth hospital / Dr Edwin HO disappeared once I confided in him that I only can pay him by instalment. I have planned my escape to run away from both hospitals stay for fear of mounting debts, simply I cannot pay them! Angioplasty can wait. My family need to be taken care of and that is all in my head and I cannot rest till it resolved. A roof will do. I am totally stressed out. My heart pain was receding after taking medication and thank to GTN is tiny TNT and a life saviour pill to keep me alive till date. Former Minister MAH Pow Tan of Ministry of National Development /MND responded to my appeal letter and Housing Development Board /HDB informed me for selection of an unit flat where is now our permanent abode that we called home at last but with due sacrifices. My wife took up a job as Dental Assistant with take home pay hardly can make ends meet but we strive on. I would hunt for cheapest "Do It Yourself" /DIY on offer. Anything from kitchen cabinets to wardrobes, lightings to power points, painting, laying vinyl flooring, etc. that essentially help the makeover just good for living-in comfortably. Using carton boxes, big books, shoe boxes to stack up and placing the DIY cabinet without fully assembled on top of it to exact and mark the positioning of the required height and drill holes on the wall to mount the DIY wall cabinets, I would use my head to push up the DIY wall cabinet (not fully assembled) to pinch exactly and positioning for wall drilling. I done it singlehandedly and my dog Joddi would understand head can be of other use. She would hide herself in my son's room when I start drillings. I have to work to complete the bare essential makeover on even days. I have to see to my health not to over work. My heart decide. I can do more on good day and I rested in between man hours so not take risk for another heart attack. How did I survived multiple heart attacks; thanks to GTN with these tiny white tablet works like miracle. It works effectively well under the tongue and will numb the whole body. I can felt the pressure rushing thru my body and knock me off, fallen asleep next I awoke with heavy head and body weakness. I have grown to be dependent of such medicines and its abusive side effects had taken toll to my other parts of the body and become a chronic illnesses with related ailments just like badly rearrangement of archaic atoms. First on list is high blood pressure, a pre-diabetic sufferer, genetically proven and inherited an ischemic heart disease, disease of the digestion system- Helicobacter pylori (H. pylori) digestive tract digestive diseases, psoriasis-skin disease (sensitive skin) then mild stroke from previous heart attacks left rampant trace of other body malfunction only to the left side of my body from head to toe; ringing ear, dizzy spell, poor vision, muscle weakness, weak kneel and joints-slow locomotion. Persistent coughing, foul breath from oesophagus tracts and bowel gas/break wind uncontrollable due to daily medicines intake causing a storm inside my stomach. It is okay I have Electronic Road Pricing /ERP inside the body in control that last 1hr of traffic congestion. I am not beneath choice but of financial constraint that I need to abandon costly medicines especially the heart. From Traditional Chinese Medicine /TCM $13/ packet, for gastro 1 tablet costing from $3.50 now $5.00 or more. I can buy a loaf of bread for $1.60 that fed my family for 5 days. Frozen fishes for $1.20 cheapest in Singapore! I am worried the cost of staying alive. Generic medicines take me to see another day as what was yesterday tomorrow but it would not cure me for a sunset paradise. My body had housed to all these generic beings over 29 years. My immune level is lower by days as I grow older. I am sensitive to allergen airborne. Aggressive food is a no. Of course I must find economic healing foods yet affordable so I could die a happy death. I am into pure distilled water intake so pure that I feel holy, real hard rice ($6/5kg vs $13/700gm for bird seeds – I can live longer by the cost, not because of my impotency but to straighten my gut, potatoes high in energy stuff to ease my daily bowel, cauliflower a size of my brain to ease my bowel so to think afresh, carrot, cabbage altogether a good source of fat removal plus onions (an oriental wasabi delight), turmeric, blue ginger, old ginger and lemongrass for a complete detoxification with double certainty and twice blessed. Agile joints will keep me going for another 100 years!

BAD NEIGHBOURS FEEDING ON
BAD SOCIAL HABITS…

I will be twice blessed if I can outlive my neighbour. Inconsiderate cigarette smoker, troublemaker doing cowardice acts and misdemeanours. We shut our doors closed ever since we moved in to our new HDB flat. He has a bad habit of jingling his punch of keys intentionally whenever he open his front gate and main doors. I peek thru the pin hole of my main door and saw his movement of hand holding the keys were swinging left to right and versa and no doubt he is up to no good. The neighbour would hide behind the main door rubbing his genitals which we felt disgusted and insulted. They would leave waste papers outside our premises. My small breed and a trained therapy dog (recommended by heart surgeon/Dr Chan-TTSH), Joddi would bark furiously or any dogs will bark as a natural reaction moreover their immediate instinct is to protect me the owner. I question his action and warned him to stop doing it. He made up a story to the neighbourhood police that I asked my dog to bite him. He is incredible liar and dangerous foreigner. He is worse than a snake as the Indian neighbour said. He can twist his words and somehow he made the police authority believe his side of story. The police authority came many times over to check on me or rather my dog that has caused inconvenience to my family with undue stress. The neighbour did not stop his wilful misdemeanour there and then. He got AVA authority in wanting to take away my dog for good. Of course I defend vehemently of such ill fabricated lie of my neighbour and on that day my dog did not bark at all when AVA officer came to our house simply because my dog is not being agitated. The neighbour rented out the whole flat to indifferent and wayward tenant come and go. Police authority came by to spot check on them who were been complained by other neighbours that made us feeling insecure and unsafe. Occasionally the neighbour hold prayer rites by burning incense that smother with thick fume so suffocating that force us to take refuge downstairs. We endure for our home is here but they can make a quick exit to the next stop or back to their country when they got want they want. They know it is good to own a Singapore Passport to their future freedom getaway and have their children to study here so to gain better and quick entry elsewhere.

It is most hurting when the neighbour said to me "your government need us more than you" is it to spike me or just an intimidating stance? I truly support foreign talents and happy to say I have managed to convince them to take up Singapore citizenship. They were specialized in radio frequency, power transmission and thermal technology but not those who are spoiler to destabilize our stable social framework that we have mustered it during our LKY's era. The 1960s upheavals were still remain vivid in my mind and learn not to have it at all costs for many generations to come.

MY WIFE THE VICTIM...

In 2000s. My wife "GSK" joined Messrs: Dr Marcus Cooney and Associates at Tanglin Shopping Centre. She was a Dental Assistant. Her take home pay barely can make end meets. We live frugal without qualms. It is not easy to use word to describe her as a person. Innocence is the closest and only fair word why? She attended her boss/Dr TOH CHIN WEE's wedding dinner. The eldest brother Dr TOH CHIN CHYE /former deputy PM asked my wife "GSK" "who is the prime minister of Singapore" She said "I do not know" Dr TOH laughed heartily. It is on the TV news of the Boris Johnson in BREXIT affair. She would ask "Isn't he the guy who acts in the movie "Dumb Dumber" so Innocence as it is. Having conversation like "every little things is cute" & her impromptu reaction "getting old is disgusting" as she looked at herself and I laughed. I find her amusement harmless and were in good ways. She is soft spoken, gentle and get frighten easily (medically & genetically her heart is weak), timid of a fair lady traits. But she is very particular about hygiene and cleanliness especially in her working area. Any messing-up her working place, her face will show. She is hard working, quick with her nimble hands that made her uniquely versatile. She is fast learner and picks up all those basic things that she needs to know about dentistry in a short time. She can assist up to 5 to 6 dental cases seamlessly and never run late in fact finish early that makes her the favourite nurse among the dentists especially the (Australian citizen and Singapore PR) employer Dr Cooney has reserved praise for her exceptional and efficient dental assisting. She was rewarded with twice incremental pay rise and given twice bonuses yearly that saw many her colleagues envied. Dr Marcus Cooney is a generous person and known to the community of his volunteering service in rendering help to the needy of the poor countries. Her wife Ms Angela works alongside him in the clinic to oversee the daily operation. They have two lovely children. A boy and girl. Their good merits bestow good karma. Ms Diana was the 1st manager. She likes my wife for her obvious good work ethnics and hand skills that enable an efficient workflow and render dentists to attend more dental cases. Once she starts work she will be busied like a bee. She always arrives at work as early as 7.30am. We woke up 5.30am every day and start the day with daily prayer. "Blessings - home and away" then clock struck 6am alert to Our National Anthem on TV even Joddi the dog knows our routine well. Bread and hot coffee for breakfast and packed her lunch box of yesterday leftover food for my wife "GSK". The traveling time from home to workplace is around half an hour to forty five minutes. It was a routine hand in hand every day and we did not take for granted for 18 years. Those moments we shared, taking the train together, observing people making their way thru the pack, funny how they and us all seem to do the same each day by the week and year make us no different from ants. The clinic opens at 8.45am. She will set up the treatment room. Dentists do take her for granted to do more than nurse job scope as stipulated to more of a domestic helper of errand works, cleaning soiled shoes or dress for the dentist, fetching newspaper, making beverage drink, even using hair dryer blowing dentist hair dry, play nanny for their children, etc.

* 1) there're instances where my wife was been shouted at with demeaning words, derogatory remarks and humiliations that she felt deeply hurt "No overtime No Money for you!"- Female dentist "L" and "work with a Monkey" – male dentist "G". Both are

husband and wife dentists working together in the same clinic. Female dentist "L" would berate and belittle my wife whenever her mood changed yet always foul mood. Male dentist "G" would force my wife to stand on castor chair to clean the window panes

at 14th floors without concern of her safety and moreover my wife was the only nurse ordered to do such window cleaning hence both said dentists had abused their authority thus committing **Professional misconduct**.

* 2) Male dentist "G" used the narrow passage way as a pretext to make bodily contact with my wife "GSK" as she was carried a tray of instruments with both hands and it is difficult to manoeuvre out of the tight spot from the narrow passage way. The male dentist "G" would coerce "you go first' and remain at the same spot. The male dentist "G" could have excuse himself and go inside to his room instead. It happens one time too many. The male dentist "G" would leave his room door ajar so he can peek thru the door gap to see and target whether my wife is making her way along the passage way so he can make his move to intercept and repeat the same pretext as mentioned. My wife "GSK" was startled to such repeated dentist "G" act and take precaution to avoid and not to fallen prey again. My wife "GSK" spotted him of making such misdemeanour time and again. Going to changing room is also a nightmare because the same dentist "G" would use pretext to take his cup and bash into room while female nurses were in the midst of changing (pantry room for changing) without warning or knock on the doors.

* 3) Dentist "G" used soiled tissues and empty boxes to throw at my wife "GSK" buttock. Dentist "G" used rubber bands to shoot at my wife's thigh and buttock (such incident brought up at the nurses meeting chaired by company director male dentist Siew, general manager Suzanne and nurse manager Tracy all present. The director male dentist Siew remarked "just playing"). Male dentist "G" is a habitual stalker who set right in front or next to my wife "GSK" as pretext and munch disgusting words (nobody wants to talk to me, I'm a nagger, I'm not a man) to irritate while

eating during lunch time even to the extent of asking too personal things, "how to give birth?".

* **4)** The male laboratory technician "N" is another predator to prod inappropriately with his both left and right fingers at both sides of my wife body above the bra line from behind more than one occasion. My wife "GSK" was alarmed and shocked. These happen when my wife was alone having lunch in the pantry room or doing stock checking, bending forward to count stock, or walking along the narrow passage way and the male lab technician "N" always strike from behind. My wife "GSK" did bring up to the manager Tracy and boss Dr Cooney but to no avail.

* **5)** The male lab technician "N" touched the female nurse buttock with both hands from behind but she dares not complain for fear of losing her job.

***6)** The male lab technician "N" forcibly intimidated my wife "GSK" to the corner and so close that my wife "GSK" cannot make way to escape. *The general manager "S" chided my wife for over sensitive or citing that they are just playful, showing unconcern, disinterested and deviate from the subject matter and take no action. My wife felt dejected and insecure.

*The 1st manager, Ms Diana resigned and was replaced by Ms Warren Tracy who was a junior nurse. She was a newly appointed manager. She was my wife's nemesis. My wife "GSK" come to know that she is a transgender thru female colleagues encounter. She favours more to her same kind. The manager "T" would make issue out of proportion and always denial when confronted or seek to clarify. The manager "T" can change her words at whims. Manager "T" would belittle and humiliate my wife in front of junior staffs and new recruits. Hence their attitude towards my wife was not helpful in working harmoniously thus no respect for the senior. They do not follow the clinic standard protocols and do what they like let alone respect for my wife "GSK". My wife "GSK" took this up to the boss/employer Dr Cooney but again it resurfaces and matter repeated. My wife "GSK" bears with it only then suffer in silence as she needs the job badly. She been chided off of being overly sensitive or pass it off as they were just playing. *GM "S" takes up matter of childish nature like not talking, eating alone, even being quiet and harmless banter things with colleagues made into big issues. GM"S" takes favouritism as she pleases.

* 7) Her favourite nurse made big mistake and took no responsibility let alone accountability that the incident caused flooding in the clinic and soiled the floors which took days to clean up by the cleaning contractor yet the GM "S" said to her "it is okay, dear!" but my wife "GSK" only turned off the wrong switch and was berated aggressively, forced my wife to relate her mistake in the group chat thus shaming her (act of discrimination and abuse). The highlights of incidents as I took note of its happening as I dictate like a jigsaw puzzle when my wife "GSK" starts to confide in me as she relates and recalls her misery in pain and ask "Why me?" and she weeps. There were physical abuse namely male laboratory "N" & dentist "G" that are amounting to sexual harassment are of criminal offence punishable by Laws but the company/management takes no action and allows the predators to do more harm to my wife "GSK". My wife is working under such precarious & toxic environment with no protection at all. My wife has grown to fear of the said predators might strike again. In overtime such fear developed and induced psychological stress at work.

The boss/employer Dr Cooney left the company for good. His flustering health after the operation has kept him out from clinic activity and recuperating back home in Australia. He travels to Singapore barely seldom. There were setbacks in business and in red. Structural changes to the management and GM "S" has more of the say now than before. One after another about 5 personnel including associates dentists who generate more money for the company and stay in black for many years and make good of the profit to expand to a bigger premises in Camden Medicals. They were the pioneers with Dr Cooney since the clinic inception

1997s (was a great blow to Dr Cooney), either senior or long serving staff were asked to leave abruptly. They left the company are not on their free will or on their own accord. The way of execution leading to dismissal is questionable beyond doubt led to staff gossip of staff on away leave GM "S" told staff named Kate not to come back to work or drastic cut to staff named Sarah salary is a no option for her to return to work. My wife "GSK" was next of such victim. What is mean to GM "S" or company for a staff who works for 18 years with pioneer status do not deserve careful consideration in all circumstances than warrant a straight red carded suspension? What about her 18 years of valued contribution to the company growth thru hard work and doing more to assist in overtimes when other nurses refused and in working during weekends on emergency cases notwithstanding the sacrifices of quality time with family? My wife "GSK" gives it all wholeheartedly for 18 years and never ask for pay rise because my wife "GSK" believes "hard work begets reward when due". With 18 years in a company even a plant slowly has taken roots to grow more of a tree let alone when seedling processes take essence of time longer, it takes more than care to flourish life in it. It is cruel to chop the tree down without any good reason only with evil motive. My wife "GSK" has given her devotion and unyielding love in rendering service to the company. She merely asks a decent livelihood to have foods to feed her family in return. The whole end to end episodes are premeditated leading to wrongful suspension. The plying craft towards my wife's suspension started quickly when all the senior managers and the boss/employer Dr Cooney were no longer with the company. They have clear insight to all the incidents and happenings to my wife "GSK" and also the dark side of it. The introduction of 5 leaders was causing disharmony and creating factions among the staff. The power play in the guise of work to disadvantage staff and those vulnerable will be fallen prey. Making life difficult for the targeted nurse to run about in assisting from room to room and 8 floor to 14 floor in frustration and overstress. Any signs of disagreement from the targeted nurse the leader will make it an issue to GM "S". The A to Z moves were to get rid of my wife "GSK". It is uncommon as GM "S" and the company/management put in place an immediate replacement whom was an ex-staff and used to talk to my wife "GSK" but she kept a distant and very unkindly sort of person. As the days loom and feeling was not right all around my wife "GSK" only way was to stay inside the room during lunch time to avoid unnecessary trouble, occupied her time during office hours to help out at the back up area, doing area cleanings and washing the fridge. She avoids gossiping and even having her lunch at the step of the fire escape staircase outside the clinic still she is targeted a scapegoat for other nurse mistakes. Accumulative incidents (1 to 7) as mentioned above right up to the recent company

*8) Using the Company Annual Dinner and Dance, treating my wife "GSK" as an outcast was obvious to deflate my wife's "GSK" morale knowing my wife "GSK" is in need of money.

*9) The annual company monetary gift or red packet or locally called "Ang Pow" Chinese New Year 2018 Incident to take away the rightful fixed amount entitled for my wife "GSK" which was pre-set by the boss/Dr Cooney for every Chinese New Year red packet giveaway and give it to her favourite staff instead was clearly to spite and anger my wife "GSK".

*10) Incident of Annual Year End Staff Appraisal around December which every staff looks forward to increment pay rise after their appraisal but only my wife "GSK" was left out. Staff take this chance to say petty things against each other that of the past to have a good return in the increment or playing the tune to please GM "S". My wife "GSK" was expunged from staff list even before the suspension was served was indeed clear cut attempt of constructive dismissal.

*11) Both predators the male lab technician "N" and dentist "G" step up the frequency of stalking on my wife along the corridor/passage way even at bus stop outside to put mounting pressure as an attempt in ousting my wife "GSK" prior to the suspension. The

suspension is one sided proceeding, unfair, discrimination, bias and prejudice hence unlawful. My wife 'GSK" was not given her legal right and opportunity to defence as to why she should not be suspended and dismiss vigorously the wrongful and false accusation of violent and threat conduct.

Those incidents namely 1 to 11, against my wife "GSK" as mentioned above are by far greater in term of severity have had inflicted more harm to my wife "GSK" amounting injury to her mental health than barely ballpark those ill words of "violent and threat" which are utterly unfounded and baseless as captioned in suspension letter. Why they are not neither sanctioned nor reprimanded or given suspension??? It is unspeakable to a dental industry which promotes utmost care but not to my wife "GSK" in anyway. Obviously my wife "GSK" is the victim of discrimination and abuse at workplace.

* 12) Evident that the action of female dentist Stephanie slammed the cardboard doors so loud that every staff got shocked and repeatedly slamming it when every staff question of her wrongdoing was not even reprimanded or suspension taken against her of violent conduct. It clearly shows that my wife "GSK" suspension is of discriminatory and unlawful thus abused.

On the fateful day which was also the last day to grace the Chinese New Year 2018 and usher the beginning of the year of Pig. The boss/Dr Cooney himself was missing CNY celebration which was marked as his departure for good. Every Chinese surely are in jolly mood to celebrate abd having dinner together with the family but not my wife "GSK". My wife "GSK" was having lunch at the pantry room where everyone was there. The GM "S" shouted sternly "You come to my office". My wife "GSK" was taken aback and dumfounded. My wife "GSK" was still at lost and went into GM "S" office to see both her permanent dentist "D" and GM "S" with stone-face, stretching their back against the chairs and sitting crossed legged. GM "S" asked my wife "GSK" "take the letter and go home". Even GM "S" continue to insult my wife "GSK" in contemptuous way. GM "S" said "you can come for the nurse meeting". Here the GM "S" barred my wife "GSK" from coming to work and getting a kick out of it by telling my wife "GSK" to go back for nurse meeting. It is too much humiliating! And GM "S" contradicted herself always. There again GM "S" has mislead my wife "GSK" countless times as to supposedly review the findings with my wife "GSK" in her present but nothing happen and make my wife 'GSK" to sign the second suspension letter without a word of enlightenment whatsoever, just said "go away" after my wife "GSK" stood there and kept waiting for instruction. GM "S" shows no positive actions and been evasive to mislead thus committing **professional misconduct**. Her behaviour towards my wife "GSK" is like "water and oil'. GM "S" is not a good person who can offer help needless to say to explain clearly beyond any doubt as to what is suspension to a simple minded woman so to my wife "GSK". My wife "GSK" indeed needs positive action cum professional guidance in this exceptional circumstance and failing which GM "S" has committed **professional misconduct** in all counts. To my wife "GSK" is just an ordinary employee and all her life my wife "GSK" understand is to work. My wife "GSK" tried to apprehend as she never come across "suspension" in her entire career. She paused and did not really read as she was lost but rushing thru the word "violent" "threat" in the letter. My wife "GSK" picks from there and said to GM "S" that "smack or slap you" was just passing banter and harmless exchange where her colleague said to her first and my wife "GSK" reacted playfully by saying back to her. It is very obvious that GM "S" makes it up as an issue out of proportion coupled with the discrimination act of shouting at my wife GSK" in front of everyone during lunch in the pantry room prior to going to the GM "S" office is a clear evident to demoralize, humiliate and in attempt openly in getting rid of my wife "GSK" as quickly as possible. In so doing the GM "S" has committed **professional misconduct**. My wife "GSK" was choking and fighting back her tear and crying even pleading that she needs the job. Both GM "S" and her permanent female dentist "Diana" were flippantly unmoved and unfazed by my wife "GSK" impassioned plea. My wife "GSK" permanent dentist Diana cannot be involved so do the other female dentist Chia in any capacity in the suspension proceeding because the rule of neutrality stand which due involvement infringe the labour law practices therefore committing **professional misconduct**. Why was not the Group Human Resource called upon to handle such matter? Why was Group Human Resource NOT involved? To suspend an employee must act above boards, made known the basic facts and deliberate beyond any reasonable doubt thus all were absent. Moreover the law stated clearly suspension cannot exceed **7 days**. But my wife 'GSK" was suspended for **14 days** and GM "S" had mislead my wife "GSK" is also committing **professional misconduct**, My wife "GSK" was not given her legal right to defence as to why she should not be suspended and to dismiss vigorously the wrongful and false accusation claim as appended in the suspension letter of "violent" and "threat" which are indeed baseless and unfounded. Since GM "S" shown no interest in helping, my wife "GSK" did ask to seek appeal to parent company/Qualitas – Malaysia based as last resort. GM "S" replied conceitedly with a sly smile "you can try!" My wife "GSK" was indeed badly hurt and deeply demoralized. She cried as she cannot control or stop from thinking those dreadful incidents.

Our mood was dented but still our family have a feast for three plus a doggy to grace the final day of Chinese New Year 2018 for good tidings. It is Year of the Pig. I told my wife the fortune teller appeared on the CNY TV show should be shot because he mentioned those born in the year of pig will get promoted. My wife was born the year of Pig. My son and I laughed but my wife kept silence to herself. She was sad and her world plummeted. It is never before she is choking her tear as she fights to talk. Her ebullient self was not there anymore like her very own inventive lingual injected during in the casual and impromptu conversation. "Mountain tortoise" "Kang Chiong spider" "sensitive butterfly" were missing. How a deadly letter can harm so much to my wife. She utterly felt she was been betrayed by the company especially the GM "S" using a piece of letter of suspension dated 1/03/2018 -

2/03/2018 to 8/03/2018 further extended to 16/03/2018 to ruin and destroy my wife reputation and morale, self-esteem, dignity, integrity and brought about injury to my wife's mental health that require costly specialists care and follow up treatments of psychologist and psychiatrist.

06/03-07/03/2018 – I wrote emails to Qualitas Medical Group / Chairman/Managing Director - Dato Dr Noorul Ameen in seeking appeal on behalf of my wife of the wrongful suspension and her employ for 18 years with the company. The Chairman replied that he will look into the circumstance.

https://youtu.be/3B2jRjgfcLs - My wife was very depressed, not able to eat any food and unable to take the blow due to wrongful suspension. Inevitably she has taken ill. She was experiencing low mood, developed anticipatory fear and unable to sleep. She was at lost and pacing around the house. She knelt and cried uncontrollably. It pains me deeply to witness how my wife was going thru such agonising pain and it's real. Her pain cut me deeply like a knife and how I wish I can bear her pain. All I can do being her husband is to do more now than before the loving-care. I kept vigil, stay close by her side constantly and make sure that she will not do something extreme in taking her own life! I cannot let her die now because she is my life and I will be gone too. There is so much to live for especially for our family as I whispered to her. "You must live" asking my wife to return the same favour that was the fateful moment I was almost gone for good due to heart attack not once but multiple. She cried out to me "you must live, we need you and our son still young..". I am 64s then coupled with my flustering health and other woes needed to be resolved plus daily household responsibilities and with my wife sudden psychological trauma cum anxiety attacks had put me overly stressed. I have to take thing one step at a time. My wife's life is far more important than anything else. We always hope to die a happy death. I recalled the time when I was remanded at Institute Mental Health hospital for 1 month. The ordeal was torturing and frightening. Inmates or sufferers can gone berserks without warning. They eat their own poo, rubbing their genitals as they going around in circle, eating the mattress foam and banging their heads against the walls are not a good place to live. They were wrestled down by 6 or more guards and locked up in an isolated cell with heavy sedation. They were released after few days and allow to mingle in the main hall with the pack and they look pale face like zombies. The remnant sedation effect in their bodies was not totally subsided. They slurred as they talk. Even how comical their actions and funny fumbling body movement I cannot laugh at their pain of what they were going thru. I have bad flashback and scary nightmares every night of flying headless body, dark tunnel with no ends, caught by strange monster, cannot escape from captivity are the worse experience in my life. I cannot let my wife to succumb to what I have gone thru the phantasmagorias and stop her whatever I can from heading towards an irreversible end then life will be extinguished. I must constantly stay close to her. I must not allow her to be agitated. I must take her to places where she can feel positive energy like places of worship. I must build up her appetite so she can feel life, I cook to her liking. I must assure her that she is not alone. I must remind her that miracle take time and be patience. I must contain her fear by telling her I am always right here to protect her. I must give her hope by reminisce our past, gentle courtship, songs we both enjoy, how we overcome objections to have a family together, holding our only son with our embraced arms when all hope is fading, we will have a good ending when our time is up, to die a happy death. My wife was then receding bit by bit thus responding but still emotionally with anticipatory fear remain:-

13/03-15/03/2018 — I follow up emails to Qualitas Country Head / Mdm Melissa Ng Ai Kiang about my wife's 18 years of employment history, the causes of workplace harassment, discrimination acts related incidents and happenings involved my wife, repeated victimization no help whatsoever and how the wrongful suspension has somehow caused my wife stress cum duress and inevitably my wife was taken ill.

15/03-16/03/2018 – Qualitas Country Head /Madam Melissa Ng Ai Kiang replied that she will make arrangement to have face to face meeting with my wife in attempt to resolve the said matter but never materialised.

16/03/2018 – My wife felt sick after dinner in fact she did not eat well for the past weeks. She felt chest tightness and wanted to vomit. I brought her down to consult neighbourhood doctor - Health First Family Clinic / Dr Alan Lee Chi Keong. I told the doctor of the sexual harassment at workplace, low mood and not eating. Dr Alan Lee refer my wife to see a psychiatrist. Dr Alan Lee whispered to me that my wife was experiencing psychological trauma and must look after her closely because of suicide tendencies inhibit. My wife was given medication and medical leaves (16/03/2018 – 19/03/2018). The medical bill = $48.10

19/03/2018 – I accompanied and escorted my wife to see the specialist at Mind Care Clinic / Psychiatrist - Dr Emily Ho Chui Ling. I told the psychiatrist about the bad experiences as my wife confided in me as to what she encountered in her workplace. My wife was unable to talk because once she starts to talk about those incidents happened in her workplace she would cry. The psychiatrist said that my wife is suffering from depression and experiencing trauma episodes. I was told to stay close to her and engaging in light-hearted talks to take her mind off from the bad happenings. My wife was given psychiatric medicines and next appointment was 01/04/2018. She was medically unfit dated (19/03/2018 – 01/04/2018) and medical bill = $302.00

20/03/2018 – My wife started to vomit because of the psychiatric medicines and not able to eat even liquid food. I have to immediately rush her to Singapore General Hospital - Accident and Emergency because my wife felt icy cold sensation all over her body and kept shivering. We waited for 2 hours or so to see the on duty A&E doctor - Dr Michelle Mei Yi. She said my wife is going thru an anxiety attack which triggered from the psychological trauma and asked to continue taking the psychiatric medicines. My wife wanted to rest at home than being admitted for further observation. She was discharged the same day (20/03/2018 – 20/03/2018). Medical bill = $121.00

21/03/2018 - I wrote an email to Mind Care Clinic/psychiatrist – Dr Emily Ho to inform her about my wife sudden anxiety attack and vomiting after taking the medicines and to know what can be done to stop it from happening again. 22/03/2018 – Mind Care Clinic/Dr Emily Ho replied my email that my wife need to take the medicines, try to swallow the medicine and eat whatever she can.

24/03/2018 - My wife was experiencing the icy cold sensation running thru her body and this time the chest tightness that she felt accompanied difficulty in breathing. I quickly took her to Singapore General Hospital A&E but we were told by A&E staff that the long queue could take up to 6 hours wait so we took a taxi to Mount Alvernia Hospital A&E. My wife was attended by Dr Chu Chun Hong. She was wheeled to take blood test, ECG and next station for X-ray. Dr Chu said that my wife is dehydrated and nurse finds it difficult to draw blood from my wife vein. She was given appointment to consult their hospital heart specialist and psychiatrist. We were at the hospital from dusk to dawn. My wife do not want to stay in the hospital for further observation. Medical bill = $292.20 + $295.32 = $587.52

29/03/2018 - I made out another urgent email to Mind Care Clinic/Dr Emily Ho of my wife about another episode of anxiety attack and what happened at Accident and Emergency at Mount Alvernia Hospital. Also worry as to what would happen to my wife if her condition deteriorate? Would she be admitted at Institute of Mental Health hospital for stay in treatments? In the email seeking the psychiatrist in allowing for instalment payment plan.

02/04/2018 - I brought my wife to Mind Care Clinic to consult the Psychiatrist Specialist / Dr Emily Ho Chui Ling in wanting to have medicines which were least effect that induce vomiting, recede chest pain and icy cold sensation. Dr Ho noticed that my wife has lost weight and "stay close to her" was something alarming. My wife was asked to rest at home for 1 month dated (02/04/2018 – 01/05/2018). Dr Ho also wrote a letter to my wife's company / Smilefocus to inform that she is medically unfit for 1 month. We left the clinic and I have posted the letter of same by normal mail postage (30cents). Medical bill = $214.00

11/04/2018 – We were unable to pay the psychiatrist / Dr Emily Ho's costly specialist charges and reached the limit allowable from utilizing Central Provident Fund /Medisave account so we consulted Ang Mo Kio Polyclinic. My wife was referred to Tan Tock Seng Hospital to follow up treatment. Medical bill = $13.20

11/05/2018 – Making impassioned plea to Deputy Prime Minister Mr Tharman Shanmugaratnam for assistance and help. I was told to seek My Member of Parliament Madam Indranee Rajah of the same.

18/05/2018 – I wrote a detailed email to Qualitas Medical Group / Chairman regarding my wife's medical conditions caused by the wrongful suspension as above and substantiated with medical documents. Highlights those areas of concern to be readily addressed in view of my wife's safe working environment and protection. No reply whatsoever till date clearly put us in quandary to all our email attempts as mentioned was wasted and felt mislead at the top and suppressing information that of important pertinent to help my wife most readily. My wife "GSK" is clearly was constructively dismissed as mentioned above and unlawful dismissal beyond any reasonable doubt because my wife "GSK" was medically unfit and on medical leaves.

23/05/2018 – I follow up another email to Qualitas Medical Group / Chairman to elaborate the impact brought about wrongful suspension that had caused to my wife. To reassert the incidents and happenings that victimized my wife under duress with mounting pressure intensified prior to the suspension. Enclosed relevant document and medical proof in substantiation. No response whatsoever,

23/05 - 24/05/2018 – Tripartite Alliance for Dispute Management (TADM) informed that we have to submit the relevant and supporting documents on 31/05/2018 for the outstanding salary claim.

28/05/2018 – My wife and I rushed down to Tan Tock Seng Hospital - Accident and Emergency / Dr Fifi Gho Yong Xi for the same episode. She was undergone the emergency tests and discharged the same day. My wife refused to have further tests because she afraid that the hospital bills will incur heavy debts on us like previously at Mount Alvernia hospital. Medical bill = $120.00

11/6/2018 – We decided to seek our Member of Parliament for Tanjong Pagar's Group Representation Constituency (GRC) / Madam Indranee Rajah for assistance and help in regards to my wife's wrongful suspension. I briefly explained to the MP of what my wife has gone thru and victim of sexual harassment, discrimination at workplace and related matters of similar concern. MP told us that it is unlawful dismissal when an employee is medically certified sick and on medical leave.

18/06/2018 – We email to Tripartite Alliance for Dispute Management (TADM) /Madam Joey Neo to inform her that we have our meeting with Mdm Chew dated 31/5/2018 and submitted all the required documents as stipulated. She also arranged for us to consult the Pro Bono Legal Aid Clinic dated 7/6/2018. We also informed the same that we have consulted Meet-the People-Session Member of Parliament Madam Indranee Rajah of Tanjong Pagar Group Representation Constituency (GRC) of same pertinence.

19/6/2018 – We email with attached letter of appeal to Ministry of Manpower / Minister in-charge Madam Josephine Teo of my wife wrongful suspension from work, detailed background, related incidents and happenings and victim of sexual harassment at workplace.

20/06/2018 – We received email from Tripartite Alliance for Dispute Management (TADM) / Madam Joey Neo to inform us about the mediation session dated 25/6/2018 and to bring along the relevant document to support my wife's claim. No officer contact us on unfair dismissal as per email suggested.

21/06/2018 – We received email from Ministry of Manpower / M/s Seah Simin in regard to our letter of appeal to Minister in-charge Joesphine Teo to remind us to proceed the scheduled mediation dated 25/6/2018 and only then she can follow up as what course of next action we should take.

22/06/2018 – We were quite confused as to who is the person in-charge or relevant authority that we were supposed to liaise with in regard to unfair/wrongful suspension, my wife fallen victim of sexual harassment, claiming of medical bills incurred so we email to Tripartite Alliance for Dispute Management (TADM) / Mdm Joey Neo for advice.

24/06/2018 – We email to Tripartite Alliance for Dispute Management (TADM) / Madam Joey Neo to follow up as per previous email and highlight of my wife medical condition still under duress with depression and anticipatory fear due to anxiety attacks episodes of the wrongful suspension coupled with been fallen victim of sexual harassment at workplace.

25/06/2018 – I accompanied my wife to Tripartite Alliance for Dispute Management (TADM) for mediation session. The Mediator / Madam Joey Neo told us that as of today session will only be salary claim matter. She took us by surprise to make inquest of the suspension matter. GM "S" said "it's only suspension and not dismissal" as she told my wife. The Group Human recourses manager from parent company was also present. While my wife tried to relate as to how she was falsely suspended and not given the opportunity to defence and same time dismiss the claim of violent and threat were baseless and unfounded. The GM "S" at this juncture she nudged back her chair in show of disapproval and in a way subject my wife's psychological intimidation. My wife is not sound medically and she is still recovering from the psychological trauma cum anxiety attack episodes due to the wrongful and prolong suspension thus she is vulnerable to undue stress plus psychological agitation and easily upset. She is emotionally frustrated thus very much depressed. My wife begin to shed tear and cry because all the parties involved in the mediation session including the mediator are insensitive to my wife who is medically ill. She is recovering from depression and psychological trauma. Moreover the company representatives especially the GM "S" will have a go at my wife whenever opportune rise. GM "S" was in denial and that get my wife very upset. They should spare a thought for the sufferer who cannot control emotion pain that carried suicidal tendencies. My wife is beginning to feel the icy cold sensation. I have to accompany her out of the room and follow her as she paces herself along the walkway. She set down and told me she is not feeling well. The mediator came up to us and I told her that I need to rush my wife home to take her medicine to stop another anxiety attack. My wife now barely skin and bones only weighing 30s kg!, a big contrast will shock whoever know her. It is cruel to travel 15km for lost hope and walk long distance all the way to Tripartite Alliance for Dispute Management (TADM) for a wasted trip. Both of us are medically unwell in circumstances and we still hoping for a hope in getting there. What we get in return not to mention my wife was subjected to another humiliation from the GM "S". The mediator said "our case hold no water" was to imply we have no chance at all. I said that "there're more to it than meet the eyes". How thoroughly was the case deliberated to come to conclusion of "our case hold no water?" Where are the fact findings to present to us as we were eager to make good of it beyond doubt. To hold no water is not at all to do us any good in putting my wife those wrongs to right. We need all the help we can get by coming TADM so there is hope. In hoping that the authority can see clearer in wider perspectives readily than us as we were stranger and new to all this and because the said authority have the past cases of similar endeavour if not the same to corroborate the facts. We cannot die in vain for a reason that the case hold no water. But you will agreed there is after all a glimpse of life to be saved and can be saved why? "A life is struggling to live and fighting alone from the beginning of the onslaught if only you can feel every words in it". There is truth beyond doubt. Even the GM "S" knows it and slipped thru her tongue in telling my wife "too late now" then be it "18 years of employ just ended up by whim of a caption "suspension". 18 years to grind out a grit for an ordinary woman is not by chance. She stood and weather whatever come what may in work to keep her family going. She stays silence so not to laden the worry to her family. She works very hard so be rewarded that will go to the family daily bread. She is super human she can do without medical or sick leave or sabbatical leave to earn extra dollars and cents for her family that would not starve. Staff colleague alike laugh at her English proficiency and nativity but she improvises the way of working to improve productivity clearly understand how the shape of thing works. She is a precious gem gone unnoticed. She has positive energy inside out only Asperger patients feel comforting with her present. To label my wife violent and threat are not her nature or else my family will be in chaos and world upside down. We will be in and out getting summons to family tribunal court for domestic violence or history record of the same with the police authority but none at all. Those previous clinic dentists whom my wife worked with namely Dr Toh, Dr Christopher Sim and others can truly vouch for her good character or all those operators or workers simply with no particular relationship but have daily human contact with my wife and I during our usual routine of having breakfast at MacDonald, Tanglin Mall food court and Subway which are close proximity to my wife's workplace / Camden Medicals. We always chat with them in some casual exchange while we ordering and also waiting for our food, talk about ordinary life to family matter of concern and we shared then soon just a rapport developed into more of a friendship. Somewhat our lives revolt around the ordinary life people with down to earth hope. Even the security guards of Camden Medicals are the best witness of our many years in seeing us in the morning of going in the building of Camden Medicals and out after work. The elderly cleaner of 90s of age and shuttle bus driver can do us the same – "character clearance". All of them will say the same thing "we're a loving couples" why? Because we were always holding each other hands while we walk. To us it is a natural thing but there are people who do not like us holding hands. Either they have failed in relationship or broken down marriage or just cannot see people happy. They become evil doers and prey on the weak so they are happy. They do not care about comeuppance nor believe in karmic retribution.

We stated the facts as admissible evident truthfully: - A) as listed above (1 to 12) as of incidents and happenings that targeted my wife "GSK" the victim of constructive dismissal altogether under the ploy of craft or pretext of suspension of violent and threat which are totally baseless and unfounded. The suspension was totally unfair because 1) company failed to explain clearly: a) what is suspension and b) Why is suspension taken against the employee in this case my wife "GSK". The management /GM "S" as a company representative to chair and serve the letter of suspension has failed (a & b) resulting deprived the positive actions entitled to the victim my wife "GSK" hence committing professional misconduct. Moreover the victim my wife was not given the opportunity to defend vehemently as to why the victim/my wife "GSK" should not be suspended and dismiss vigorously the claim of violent and threat which were baseless and unfounded. 2) Dentist Dianne Sainsbury and dentist Francine Chia should not be involved in any circumstances due to neutrality under the labour law practice. Dentist Dianne Sainsbury was the victim/my wife "GSK" permanent dentist and also dentist Francine Chia had direct working relationship with the victim/my wife "GSK" hence such act has infringed the labour law practice thus committing professional misconduct. 3) Group Human resources dutifully responsible was not called upon to act in view of the severity and gravity of suspension had consequences namely damage to the victim/my wife "GSK" reputation & long-term impact namely psychological and emotion pain to the victim/my wife "GSK". Suspension was hell bent, globally premeditated actions with bias and prejudice coupled with discrimination cum one sided suspension deem unethical in fact wrongful. 4) No review whatsoever in the course of suspension. 5) Exceeded 7 days suspension against the labour law practice. 6) Unlawful dismissal as the victim/my wife "GSK" was medically certified unfit from (16/03/2018 to 01/05/2018). 7) Parent company/Qualitas HQ was informed and duly substantiated with all relevant documents of the victim/my wife "GSK" including letter of appeal and follow ups but parent company /Qualitas HQ mislead and suppressing information in allowing sister company /Smilefocus & GM "S" to unilaterally monopolize its execution quickly as possible to dismiss the victim/my wife "GSK" in a single stroke. 8) Both male technician "N" & male dentist "G" have had subjected the victim/my wife "GSK" grievous act as listed above (2 to 6 &11) of outrage of modesty amounting to sexual harassment punishable by law but the company/management /GM "S" and company director cum dentist "S" did not take any action but simply remarked it as "play, play only" Hence therefore the victim/my wife "GSK" has suffered long term psychological and emotion pain. The victim/my wife "GSK" kept it to herself knowing the company even the ex-boss Dr Marcus Cooney and ex-manager Tracy Warren conveniently kept it under wrap. My wife "GSK" had informed ex-manager Tracy Warren verbally and I written a letter to ex-boss Dr Marcus Cooney of such happenings.

We need to have an official transcripts of the mediation dated 25/06/2018 with parties involved Tripartite Alliance for Dispute Management (TADM) /Madam Joey Neo, Smilefocus /GM "S" and representative from Qualitas Medicals/ Madam (?) so we can deliberate with our Member of Parliament for Tanjong Pagar Group Representation Constituency (GRC) /Madam Indranee Rajah. Without which we cannot be able to proceed or take the next course of action. Till date we have not received from TADM.

03/10/2018 – My wife and I went to Ang Mo Kio Polyclinic to follow up and collect her medication. Her complaint were body and joints numbness accompanied bearable pain. Medical bill = $15.75

11/10/2018 – Tripartite Alliance for Dispute Management (TADM) / Madam Joey Neo informed of the outstanding salary claim = $3292.00 excluding $1422.57/medical bills incurred thereafter.

14/10/2018 – I written an email to Tripartite Alliance for Dispute Management (TADM) / Madam Joey Neo that it is important to address first the crux of the suspension rather than the outstanding salary claim preceded the former because undoubtedly it will enable to establish the root cause without further procrastination thus prevent undue stress to the victim/my wife "GSK". Secondly it is effectively uncover the truth and gamut of the circumstances most readily. I stated clearly beyond doubts that the important highlights corroborated with facts cum evident that we were lobbying since the beginning which we were overly concern that the suspension had indeed fraud. It has committed infringements in several aspects of non-compliance to the labour law practices as stated. I also informed the same to Tripartite Alliance for Dispute Management (TADM) with clear intent that we will be seeing our Member of Parliament for Tanjong Pagar Group Representation Constituency (GRC) /Madam Indranee Rajah for urgent advice of the aforesaid hence we need the mediation as per transcripts dated 25/06/2018 to facilitate our deliberation confidently.

I tried in all the earnest attempts to put the facts as it were so there were no shadow of doubt that my wife "GSK" was somewhat the victim of constructive dismissal. The impact of the unfair/ wrongful suspension had done considerable damage or injury to my wife "GSK" namely her credibility, integrity, dignity, reputation made good by each layer accumulated of 18 years of employ with the company were totally destroyed (her inner soul decried "where is the justice!") plus inflicted long term psychological and emotion pain with a lifelong permanent scar (this's most venomous and deadly option of an evil person's choice to execute. I have no wish to be devil advocate to say much of its related instances). The victim/my wife "GSK" is barely skin and bones just over 30 kgs, my son from (65 to 57kgs) and myself from (86 to 77kgs). Our family, all felt the same crude force of unfair/wrongful suspension caused to my wife. The unfair/wrongful suspension was indeed cruel without doubt. It is like throwing her into an open sea and letting her do her own drowning while they already celebrating by putting in place in allowing the craft of their ploys go in auto mode all for a reason in systematically fashion. Legitimately the victim/my wife "GSK" was ceased of employment. The victim/my wife "GSK" has never had such experiences because she always innocent. The depression was always there to wreck, to split the brain. She cannot fumbled to sleep no way because her body gone into overdrive, not eating and vomiting were the first sign entering into days and then weeks. Psychological trauma taken over and worked like an epic for tsunami slam and cracked up. The body felt icy cold and its sensation run every part of the body, shivering, slurring and paranoid. My wife "GSK" was battling to control or stop the anxiety attack but simply cannot because her mind was out of her control thus inviting fleeting suicidal thought most painful and fearful.

"The Mind is a jar into which space is poured. Space is the house which Consciousness is building for itself. Suffering is the cause of Consciousness & keeper of Time. Consciousness is pain. When we take pains, we take Consciousness. What we get in exchange for our pains we get in exchange for Consciousness. Consciousness is the limitation to which we are all confined. It is Consciousness that denies us Freedom, yet it is Consciousness that set us free. The desire to avoid suffering is the longing to be dead. In death there is no rest. The atoms cannot surrender to silence."

I see her in pain and the intensity I felt twice as much simply she is my wife and love of my life. My belief that Man are made to protect woman. The first instance when I see my wife in pain I felt it too. I kept her vigil whole night and grasped her hands tightly even resting. I would not leave her out of my sight. She becomes a child that I have to cajole and coerce into eating, eating and eating. I discovered the talent of lying and I become a very modest person. I lied that the medicines are different and better from the last time so my wife would take her medication and get well quickly. Before my wife could make a din I quickly apologise and promised I will be careful next time. I learned to play many roles when comes to taking care of my wife who is undergoing traumatic life change. I explained "Between the extreme edge of the Universe and the extreme centre exists nothing but the extreme." She would stare blank and giggled. I go on to tell her "The thought processes of the dinosaur were in no way inferior to Man's. Man would never have "thought" had the dinosaur thought before him. The first amphibian that crept out of the ooze was in no way inferior to the first man that leapt into the air. Nature specializes in failures. Only God is right the first time. Nature loves its failures. So do the failures. Nature eschews its roles and must deceive its failures. Nature's "successes" are failures that have not yet found the door. Nothing is permitted to rest." She quietly fallen asleep.

"Some of the most painful scars: The ones that hurt the most are the scars that can't be seen. Instead of wiping my tears, I'm trying very hard to wipe away the people who create them. Depression is a prison where I'm both the suffering prisoner and cruel jailer. Depression is lot like drowning except that I can see everyone else around me breathing. When I'm depressed I don't control my thoughts, my thoughts control me. I wish people would understand this. I knew exactly what they're doing, that's what hurts the most. When depression takes over and I can't push through it, I have to close my doors and shut the world out. It's the only way I know how to survive. I am not using my depression as an excuse. Trust me, I'd give anything to function "normally" On a day to day basis."

.....The manager constructively allows the harassment to continue. Non-intervention or inadequate interventions escalate the dissension. A virus reproduces by spreading to as many hosts as possible. **Mobbing** is like a virus that begins with two or more bullies, who quickly align with others to gang up on and force out the target.

"You never know how strong you are until being strong is the only choice you have People cry, not because they're weak. It's because they've been strong for too long. You can see many smiles every day, but you can never know whose world is actually upside down. Every time people ask me if I'm okay, it's just a reminder that I'm not I forgive a lot, but I never forget what's said and done"

*Stage 1: Instigated by a bully teasing, criticizing, and "picking on" an employee. A collaborator often joins in demeaning and shunning their target.

*Stage 2: Harassment and Stigmatization describes the us-versus-the-target tactics, with hostility increasing. The primary strategy is stigmatizing humiliation. Blaming and shaming tactics exclude the target from group activities. Damaging accusations undermine the targeted employee's abilities, confidence, and well-being. Without effective intervention, abusive behaviour escalates.

*Stage 3: The Critical Incident begins with the bullies clashing with the targeted employee, on a series of issues. Entitlement and the liberty to exclude are strong motivators. The rumour mongering discredits and humiliates the target. The objective is to collect or create evidence of "gross misconduct". A critical incident is fabricated to prove she is guilty of severe wrongdoing requiring swift managerial action - Workplace Suspension. Mobbing perpetrators are recruited through well-established networks. The ranks close ostracizing the target. Intimidation and psychological violence are pervasive to crush the contemptible outcast.

*Stage 4: Adjudication determines whether the mobbing process is intensified or stopped through hearings and/or mediation or a single meeting with senior management - none whosoever. The fundamental motivation is character assassination, with attacks on the outcast's competence and credibility. Devaluation, by management, is a powerful means of inhibiting backlash and empowering the perpetrators. Mobbing cultures crush and force out talented employees. The damaging tactics are humiliating, intimidating, and isolating. Those targeted often experience stress-induced physical and/or psychological impairments. Senior management's lack of accountability is indicated by the target and/or distressed bystanders resigning to escape the hostility.

*Stage 5: Elimination establishes the outcast's punishment. Senior management is inundated with the perpetrators' accusations. A manager faced with a group of subordinates, who get along and work reasonably well, all of whom despise another employee and want to be rid of her, ordinarily supports the collective will. Each higher level of authority is faced with overturning the will of a successively larger group of subordinates. Often the solution is elimination of the outcast. Unwarranted suspension or unjustifiable termination demonstrates senior management's failure to act in "good faith and fair dealing in the manner of dismissal.

"Depression is like a bruise that never goes away. A bruise in your mind. I just got to be careful not to touch it where it hurts. It's always there though."

- **Workplace bullying and mobbing** like all violations of human dignity don't just happen. It takes a sequence of events or an environment conducive to their development. *Avoidance and ostracizing of the target.*Petty harassment: making the target's life difficult.*A critical incident that triggers formal sanctions: "something has to be done."*Aftermath of the incident: Unwarranted Suspension & Unjustifiable Termination. Target/Mobbed Victim die of stress-induced illness, or commits suicide. Workplace bullying can start in subtle ways. Often targets are not even aware that it is happening as some types of bullies prefer to work behind the scenes to set things up for an eventual onslaught. One of these forms involves the good 'old grapevine or gossip. Bullies will start to plant the seeds of discontent and doubt about the target and begin separating them from the herd. If there is something already different about the target such as their background, qualifications or work ethic so much the better. Targets may find themselves at stage progression as they are avoided by co-workers whose minds have been poisoned against them. Once the target is no longer considered "one of us" and has become "one of them" it is easier to justify the initial harassment. The bullies and those who play along justify the harassment of the target as being somehow deserved and "brought on themselves."

Of course, some of the things being done to the target may be quite petty and they may not yet understand that they are being bullied at work. Perhaps they are not included in an invitation for lunch or a deadline for some work assignment they are working on has been arbitrarily changed at the last minute or they have been spoken to in a rude manner.

The Petty Harassment Continues. The insults, slights and rudeness continues and takes on a pattern of abuse. Targets begin to notice that not everyone is treated the same way - that they have somehow, for some reason, been selected for special treatment.

In many cases the individual instances of harassment or abuse are so petty that if one to complain to management about them they would seem ridiculous. This is the trap many fall into once they become aware of what is happening and they approach management.

Managers are presented with complaints from targets that are taken out of the larger context and are not seen as a small part of a larger pattern of abuse. They are handled piece-meal. And since each incident is so petty, so pathetic the target who is complaining about them is dismissed as a whiner who can't deal with even the smallest thing.

This is when managers, who cannot believe someone has come to them with such a ridiculous complaint, advise the target to "get over it," "deal with it," "get a tougher skin," or offer any number of other equally useless and condescending remarks.

The Target of Workplace Bullying Is Betrayed. As the harassment has escalated, the abuse become more frequent and brazen and as management repeatedly does nothing (at best) or supports the bullies, the target feels a growing sense of betrayal.

They have also been betrayed by their own sense of right and wrong. Everything they believed about how the world works has been turned on its head. They would never treat people this way, there is such a thing as right and wrong (isn't there), and what about justice and fair play! They were naive

They were betrayed by their belief that people, decent people, would never act this way in a place of work - a serious place for serious business - not a place to play petty juvenile bullying games!

They feel betrayed by management. They are, after all, the authorities charged with the responsibility to make sure the workplace is a respectful, safe and productive environment. Why do they not listen? Why do they not intervene and put a stop to such obvious abuse? Why do they dismiss my complaints and act like I'm the problem!?

"I wanted to talk about it. Damn it. I wanted to scream. I wanted to yell. I wanted to shout about it. But all I could was whisper. I'm fine. I'll be want to feel okay again. I'll be alright. One day. Someday. Just not today."

... **Psychological abuse** carried out against an employee with the purpose of making her resign her job, in the circumstances where by other means would lead to legal troubles for the employer. The employee can become a long-term victim of a series of abuses, wrongdoings and humiliation meant to force her to leave her current job. This psychological pressure should not only make her lose his position, but in most cases will also affect her health.

"Monsters don't sleep under my bed, they scream inside of my head. I hate getting flashbacks from things that I don't want to remember."

"Mobbing" is a type of systematic psychological harassment in the workplace that happens every time an employee is being harassed and stigmatized by his colleagues or superiors through gossip, intimidation, humiliation, discrediting and isolation, endangering his emotional well-being as well as his professional competence. The act of mobbing does not happen instantly. The gradual evolution of mobbing was of preparation, of slow or precipitated evolution, maturation and persistent action.

The first stage exists in every organization and does not necessarily imply the occurrence of the other steps of evolution. It manifests itself through divergences, differences in opinion or competitiveness, which is a normal phenomenon.

The second stage has elements that might trigger the occurrence of mobbing. The psychological balance of the person is somehow threatened, self-confidence is jeopardized, and stress and anxiety become a problem.

The third stage is when management should get involved. Unfortunately, most of the time this either does not happen at all, or it happens when it is already too late and the victim has already been removed. In this case, conflicts may have legal repercussions.

The final stage leads to the stigmatization, social isolation and the unwarranted suspension and unjustifiable termination from the workplace, which could make finding a new job more difficult.

Mobbing is preceded by a situation of conflict. The probability of such a situation is increased by the following factors: · deficiencies in human resources management; · organizational culture which tolerates moral harassment; · workplace instability; · personality traits of the victim; · group dynamic in the organization; · poor relationships between work colleagues; · high levels of discrimination · frequent organizational changes - situations where the manager chooses to leverage his authority when settling disputes, instead of identifying the faults in the system.

Victims of mobbing are generally dedicated to their work and eager to succeed. Despite preconceptions, the victim is most of the time job oriented with a rising career. When the first signs of mobbing appear, the victim does not fully comprehend the situation and has difficulties reacting to it.

"People who love themselves, don't hurt other people. The more we hate ourselves, the more we want others to suffer." "I would rather be a little nobody, then to be an evil somebody."

I INVOKE WHOLEHEARTEDLY:

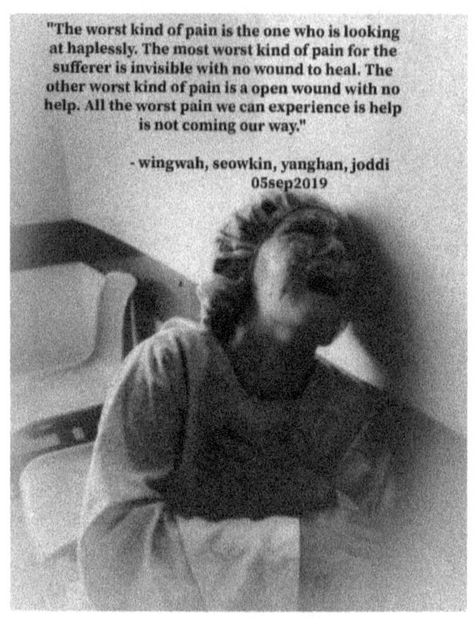

"Wherever you are, look up Seow Kin! The clouds are lifting, the sun is breaking through. We are coming out of the darkness into the light. We are coming into a new world, a kindlier world, where men will rise above their hate, their greed and brutality. Look up Seow Kin. The soul of man has been given wings and at last he is beginning to fly. He is flying into the rainbow, into the light of hope, into the future. The glorious future that belongs to you, to me, and to all of us! Look up Seow Kin look up!"

I have gained patience to her needs and wisdom to carry on that patience. It is difficult to understand pain itself because the process precedes only then can remark upon pain. Just like living is more important than life without which life cannot remarked upon. I spend more time looking after my wife.

There is no better time than now. It made no sense to some but it was logical sense right at that moment. I shut the outside world only then my wife felt safe and secure. She has developed anticipatory fear and any outside slightest noise will send her into frenzy in a way panic. I left my time to do least only after she took her medication. I too dozed off. She awoke to the bad memories still linger on so not much of a good sleep with her weary face can tell and at lost. I am sick man of the east and well medically documented with trace of chronic illnesses cum ailments. The last trail of previous multiple heart attacks has weaken my heart considerably plus subjected wear and tear as it grows older signalling me that my days in sun are foregone.

I live in a borrowed time for a reason that I still alive. It is the timely moment to rescue my wife in her darkest hours. Maybe that is the strange way of how destiny works. When time brings us together there is also time to breakaway.

Both my wife and I made a vow to die a happy death less the mundane shortcomings. As you can see the victim always suffered the pain most and why the victim is hopelessly put into such a long haul with nothing in sight, haplessly because not enough love to go around nor protection. We hoping someone will come to offer us a helping hand. We were deep in solemn prayer. Undoubtedly the case is simple and straightforward but it seems yet long and complicated because "half of the world has it all and other half of the world lie down and quietly suffered in silence".

AFTER 30 YEARS A TIMELY EXHUMATION OF MY MOTHER GRAVE...

I have a problem that weighing in my heart and mind. My mother named Madam Aw Foong Wan had been buried in Lim Chu Kang Chinese cemetery for the past 30 years. She was always a Queen of Heart to me why? I'm rebellious sort when I was young and good at running away from school. I turned to be good and well behave not because of spankings or public canings but something Mama said to me with very true sincerity which I felt it that numb all my nerves.

That moment when her tear started to roll down her cheek and glimpse of her face showing of giving up hope really torn my heart apart and she said softly "To learn One word Each day in school & that is all I ask from you" My mind went overdrive, feeling sorry, feeling guilty but it seems good deal to me.

I topped the primary six school final year exam – Tanglin Boys School. Everyone from school principal, head master, teachers to my parent felt awkwardly surprise. That okay feeling that I gave them was worthy a million or weigh in gold. Mama illuminated to me the kindliest light her world has ever known, which has endowed undying familial love, caring and humanity. Mama planted her seed of love in me. To have love to see things make living more remarkable than life. It made me not just a better person. A good soul in within. If I ever to meet my maker one day I would want to be reborn as a protector for my mama and wife once again. Mama was not a good at telling fable story. She always reminded us how tough life was living in China. Eating the bark of the tree and roots were common sight. Even deep in poverty they garnered the spirit of togetherness because there is love going around helping each other that makes China strong in within.

We were happy to have just soya black sauce spread on the rice. Mama would smash a raw egg on top the rice to the lucky birthday brother or sister. Mama remembered all 6 of our siblings' birthday. Mama cared most for the eldest brother who got the most crude force spankings from my father. Papa would grab anything from bamboo stick to belt that come handy. We were disciplined at such.

Eldest brother committed suicide when he was late 40s. He cannot handled his self-inflicted stressful life. He was an alcoholic and soon most of his organs would not survive long. My handicapped brother were spared from any punishment. He is mute and deaf born at birth. He loves to sing and the audible chords coming from his vocal was like making noise from a worn sandpapers but we all were pleased as long as he was happy. I am youngest and got the privilege to kneel for whole day as punishment than caning. I asked a lot of whys' during my childhood and I wanted to talk to someone smarter than me. Mama always return intrigue questions back at me. I was convinced then I was not that smart maybe when I reached puberty with that kind of low base tone then things will change. Parent always remind us "do not waste foods" so next life will have enough to eat and need not starve or die of hunger. To have fish and poultry on the table was a grand occasion to feast. Nothing gone to waste any leftover bones were cooked together to make soup:

"There is a spider so monstrous that in order to mate, she must spin a bauble to dangle coyly before the timid, tiny male. Enticed by such shining promise, the male scurries into her web where, stroked by her seductive legs, he copulates with this mother of his species. Their joys completed, then she consumes him, throwing away his shrivelled shell and her courting gift together. She will not have rubbish lying about her web. All males of this species are virgin. How elegantly the spider display Nature's economy and delicate sense of fun."

National Environment Agency informed of the exhumation exercise and my mother's grave was affected. I went down with my wife to take down the details needed by NEA. We travelled 15 km or more under the scorching sun. I went back home fallen sick. I consulted doctor at Bukit Merah polyclinic and given medication. I truly wanted to reunite my Papa's ashes named Chee Hock Seng was cremated at Kong Meng San Phor Kark See Monastery to be installed the niche together with my Mama's ashes at Mandai Columbarium for a good timely reunion and also be close to LKY's parent as they both long wanted. A filial piety even in ashes.

Papa was tough and robust. He run at people like charging bull. He was a bodyguard to LKY then.

I heard it over uncles chats of first hand stories about fighting, capturing of bad eggs from gangsters, secret society members to those pro-communist activists. LKY said he is good as dead meat if communists were to takeover Singapore. Papa used to come home bandaged but still carry on his routine the very next morning.

End of the month he would buy us Magnolia ice-cream that makes us very happy and favourite roasted duck as an offering to our ancestors. We have real good times together.

Come February every year. I have got both my birthday and lunar New Year to celebrate and twice blessed for the reason to lit firecrackers with pocket full of it running amok. On the eve of Chinese New Year midnight was the best treat to sync fire crackers and next day getting the feel of red carpeted everywhere from the burnt firecrackers and distinct gunpowder smell linger on. It is most happy times for the young and old.

That good old feeling can never be replaced but ended in 1972 same year Bruce Lee kicked the bucket. But Even when it comes to service for the dead, there is always a costs outlay that will incurred maybe by the hundreds if not thousands of dollar! We were in no position to pay it outright. We therefore seek the relevant authority, National Environment Agency in allowing us to pay by instalment plan. We were in no contact with our siblings since our parent demise 1990s. We were no friend only strangers.

But we only have each other in the family, my wife, seow kin, my son, yanghan, therapy dog Joddi (died up 2012s we still grief) and myself that makes us somewhat closely related to the "Adam Family".

"Man is an animal with primary instincts of survival. Consequently, his ingenuity has developed first and his soul afterwards. Thus the progress of science is far ahead of man's ethical behaviour. Nature do not need us and we need Nature"

MY SON, A SEEDLING TO A PROMISING FUTURE...

All children in some form or another have genius; the trick is to bring it out in them. I bought him a portable palm size game gadget. He mustered it and his interest withered. Now a bigger game console with Japanese language instructions still my son make it easy with no qualms and stupidity was on me. He scales up each game levels tougher as mission completed and little did he know the graphic interest so enchanting brought about in the game was slowly opening up and await him to adore in his latter endeavour.

My son Yanghan as name given by me is to stand up, be upright and useful person. He left the navy after 6 plus years stint. He done any parent proud of doing well, being top in awards. He was among the LKY's sending off navy contingent.

He is kind by nature and helpful. Because of his outgoing helpfulness he was taken a ride of totalling $20K for helping a desperado. Everyone seem to find him a modest, good jolly guy who cannot say no. He always preoccupied with his navy operation assignments round the clock and do it right the first time and get it job done most readily. He saves as he yields for study high so further an Art degree course in LaSalle Art College /Singapore. He made use of his navy gratuity to service his tuition fees knowing our family financial situation. He also works part time to defray the household expenditure. He is too had a good side of life in the navy. Probably is in the gene at work from grandpa was an architect as part of Haw Par Villa to Papa was a freelance street artist to me a transient mystic introvert art narrator to my son a perpetual graphical artist.

He is good at graphic work and quick mind that stand out in real time rendering. He gave an emotional speech at the final year at navy seminar as to how I kept pushing myself against all odds to stay survived that inspired him to do likewise in the navy whatever tasks assigned to him with no qualms whatsoever.

He will be readied for the future so it is wise not to let too much of our shortcomings to indulge in his constraint.

"Education is the path to revelation. Education is bigger than Four Letter Words. Teach the alphabet and you sow the seeds of rebellion. The free thinker travels light along the road to truth"

MY PARTNER IN QUILT WITH NO CRIME ONLY LOVE...

Our family had a dog by chance. I fetched my son after school and lunched together. We took time off to digest our fill and walk around inside a pet shop at Serangoon. This puppy was following us around, took a bow and stretched her body whenever we bumped to each other. The puppy was trying to catch our attention and we understood the puppy wanted us to adopt her. We took her home and named her Joddi. She grew to be the part of the family. She was loyal and intelligent sheltie breed. A good dog in every senses. She always stays by my side and make me happy with her doggy tricks. I bathed her every once a week. She would turn her head and look at me in a way telling me that I scrubbed too hard on her back. I have to apologise "sorry" only then I am allowed to continue. After serving her the home cooked meal and eaten, she would allow me to wipe her mouth clean then she stumbled and pressed her body against the wall as she move. Her actions never failed to amuse me and my family. It shown her appreciation cum liking of the cooked food which I prepared. Since 2008s, our family moved in to our new flat I got this neighbour living a floor up had a bad habit of throwing lit cigarette butt onto my air-con ledge. I do not understand why they send their children to school so to learn the good things yet they do not know their action of throwing lit cigarette butts into someone property is considered an arson act and fire kills lives. Another neighbour living right across on same floor has a bad habit of jingle his door keys whenever he opens his gate door. Doing his misdemeanour one time too many was a crime. My dog would bark frantically. It happened every day and I need to tell him politely "please stop". Next thing I know he complained to HDB and police authority that I asked my dog to bite him. See how these foreigner are so dangerous in words, worse than snake like the Indian neighbour said. They can twist their words. I felt disappointed that both HDB and police are on his side. I have made out a letter to Ms Serene Ng, the police superintendent /Bukit Merah Central and stated the valid points that my dog bark frantically and very loud that 3 block away can hear her barking. How can the neighbour could hear exactly those words under such noisy commotion and we were 20 ft apart that I said to my dog to bite him moreover I am carried my dog tightly to my chest and barking will drown every words I said, we were behind locked gate door and there were no act of physical intimidation. The neighbour never stop his harassment plot doing into way to get National Environment Agency / Animal Control officers to come to our house with intent to take away my dog. I made all defence to justify my dog is a good therapy dog. My dog did not bark at all when the NEA officer step into our house that prove my case. Any dog will react when disturb. Neighbour perform rites with smoky incense burning and its choking fume enter our house only to force us to leave our house to take refuge downstairs even we sealed up the door gap with Velcro would not help. Neighbour rented out the whole house with shabby tenants coming in now and then. We felt unsafe but we tolerate. I was deeply annoyed and agitated. We shut our doors to stay out of trouble. My dog, Joddi died of heartbroken.

My family and doggy were separated for a month or so for I was remanded at Clementi Police station for shop theft. Because of my both hands were handcuffed at the back had triggered a heart attack. I was rushed to Alexandra Hospital and released a few days later. There were officers coming by the hospital to take my statements. I heartily admitted taking items without paying at Ikea store. I was transferred back to Clementi Police station lock up. In the cell with painted thick walls, olden day type of water tap for drinking, wash up and below a pre-war squatting type toilet bowl.

A cell was housed to few male inmates. We were stripped bare for periodical inspection. I get to know a Chinese boy "Kenney" for phone snatch theft who wanted to be a chef as he likes making pastry. He was not in good term with his stepfather. Another cellmate with bodily tattooed Chinese teenager "Benjamin" got into illegal runner activity who wanted to be a hair stylist. He came from a home whom father and siblings were convicts and still serving their prison terms, He himself was a terror in school heydays even teachers suffered bruises. His short fuse and hot temper always got him into fights. An Indian cellmate named Pala was caught for house breaking. He wanted me to help him once my release to write to sought help from MP Ms Indranee Rajah for he was her seasoned car washer. He had a wife who would not know a thing or two about the monthly payment and settlement for monthly general household bills like utility, etc. which were accrued and accumulate mountain of unpaid bills ever since he was imprisoned. He cried out to me "no picture no sound" as he sought SOS help. I said to him:

"There's not a rich man there, who couldn't pay his way? And buy the freedom that's a high price for the poor. Poor is not a four letter words."

MIND INFIRMITY TRAPPED ONLY INSANITY RULES...

Judge Ng ordered during the pre-trail conference to have me placed 3 weeks remand at Institute of Mental Hospital for review. It is a strange place to go, not many people around and quietness made it chilling feeling. Form filling then stripped completely naked for inspection.

A cell with mattress bed lined up orderly in adjacent rows. Two male young Indian cellmates came and helped me to wrap up my allotted bed with bedsheet. Emmanuel was charged for beating up an illegal loan shark. He is agile and active and had a good appetite and ate most of my between break snacks without quilt. He loved his mother who works in Tan Tock Seng Hospital as a general cleaner. He got into fight with his brother's bad habit of taunting money from his mother. Xavier was young married man and got himself into contraband offence.

They all have loving families as I witnessed during weekend visitation. A very old grandmother with home cooked dish for cellmate "ah wei" suffering from mental illness, always pacing himself yet in his quiet moment he wanted to be a singer. He spoke highly about his sister who is a lawyer understudy. We were asked politely to have a taste of their food be it Malay, Indian or Chinese – they really bare it all and no wall between us! One or two bad eggs will find trouble but there is someone will stand up to quell it. Strange noises very nights from other cells, berserk incident of eating poo, swallow mattress foam even hanging that I have had too lived with it. Doping Valium tablets not help much still the flashbacks and nightmares of dark figures, flying headless phantasmagorias come as they will.

Here they do not expect anything different or it will be uncommon. It opens up before me a once a salient gentle mind to a greater frontier of knowing into a sphere of deep unknown not unknowable become knowable only nothingness does not exist.

My doggy died up and I still grief a week after I was released from one day in prison. I'm no stealer but still I have to pay a high price for my mistake. I have goodhearted peoples who I do not know yet they offer good gusto words to uplift, as to what I going thru. I cannot thank them more ex-Member of Parliament Mr Tarmugi, Judge Ng. Judge Roy Neighbour, Lawyer Mr Ram and Psychiatrist Dr Seetoh & Tsoi. I have fair share of good moment and it is precious always in all ways close to my heart. Heaven is kind. When life seem run deep and being cruel I got kick in the head to snap it out the dark so I can see the good light ahead. I owe too much to my Mama. Her patience, unyielding love and guidance are heavenly gift from above. For mama in her own words "To learn one word each day" I have learned it well. Now I make it a matching tribute ending credit:-

"To reach for new heights. We must continue to reach for it. One inch at a time. To make a mile of difference. We are counting steps to your Heart."

MY HEART FINALLY COME TO TERM WAY AHEAD MY MIND…

There are so much more to write about but there again I wish not to get myself misconstrued then missing the points. "I'm getting old faster mainly because of prolong dependency on five different types of long term medication excluding traditional Chinese medicines. The accompanied side effects become numb to me.

Our body is dependent on Heaven and Heaven on the Spirit. Learning acquired in youth arrests the evil of old age; and if you understand that old age has wisdom for its food, you will so conduct yourself in youth that your old age will not lack for nourishment. While I thought that I was learning how to live, I have been learning how to die.

Nature is the source of all true knowledge. Nature never breaks her own laws. I have learn to see things with my ears. Eyes to see beyond. As a well spent day brings happy sleep, so a life well spent brings happy death.

I know help and hope may not come. All is silent within my dream. But a dream lives on forever. The days and the years will go streaking by. But the time has stopped in my dream. We all have our everyday hopes and fears and you will find no exception in me. But that does not get me through a sea of tears over life's biggest tragedy. My dream still live on forever.

Both my wife and I are into last lap of our lives coupled with frail health and medical conditions that leave us a worrisome souls. We are not afraid to die and we want to die a happy death less mundane shortcomings.

Because of desperation needless to say or something tell us there is a glimmer of hope in sight we will do what an elderly couple like both my wife 60s and myself 64s to take a chance because for a tie as we born and belong here. We have been shuttling one stop to another from ministries to government agencies with quilt in seek for a timely help.

We are condemned. We have been knocking on closed doors. Hopefully until it opens we will get to know the feeling of liberation and release. With true sincerity we open up and bare the truth nothing but the truth even going into our private lives and we reveal because it shows how much the help mean to us.

Help is like oxygen that give us life without which we cannot live. How much oxygen we do not seek aplenty but good enough we take in and we will be on our way. Every help that come our way will find a place in our heart with eternal gratitude. So to be alive we know we can do more so do help that give us many possibilities. An ant life only has few days as the nature law governs. To live a day older to the ant is a bonus and to us we fight to survive. We follows nature because that is the closest way to realise and to know God. We were born in this proud land because we are blessed to have a good leader like LKY. He is with us always so do our parent's sacrifices. This is the tie nothing else even in my last breath this is still an unshaken truth. LKY brings it into our lives so to carry on with our offspring then to the next generation and beyond.

Without tie there is not a place we belong and home none at all nor a country be born. LKY's tie in the Nation flag that flies Singapore high skyward, tie in National Anthem "*MAJULLAH SINGAPURA*" that bring us together with pride, tie in Nation Pledge that we strive as an unit in diversity and tie in a land that we call Home to live and let live.

If the opposition do not have this tie is not worthy an opposition. They are just wasting their time. There are so much can be done for Singapore...I am in deep thought.

MAY THIS TIE BRING HOPE AND HELP TO US IN GODSPEED

"Despair is a narcotic. It lulls the mind into indifference If only the old and young could be the same age. It is characteristic of the nature of Ordinary Man that he imagine he is doing something hopefully new when he imitates something hopelessly old."

"Earth is full of monsters. Earth is a laboratory in which Creation toils extremely at the edge of Reality. Creation is seeking Reality. Creation specializes in Impossibility. All monsters are experiments in the form of Reality. Creation knows nothing but extremes and adores equally the virus. The forelimbs of the Tyrannosaurus Rex withered because he was not yet ready to write. These perished because they were not great enough for the future. The Hero is a monster who proves all men unequal. The Hero proves the obvious. If all men were created equal, humanity would not yet have achieved the order of the ant-heap. The savage smears the earth with blood so that his tribe may blossom and became less savage. If the savage were conservative, the arrow would still be a branch on the tree.

*It is worse to be eaten by a shark than a **Man**?"*

Above: These are hyped movies created and written novel books of the same magnitude of great interest to the masses because of its imaginative power are high in creativity and inventive in all that can grasped or uplift the senses. "WE HAVE EACH OTHER IN THE FAMILY.. if only you were there to help" as I have penned is no way near such dimension to match but as it was told in a true life happenings that revolves our lives subjected to pains and sufferings, how we take pains cum sufferings in exchange for conscious survival one step at a time. There is no help or hope in sight but we are counting steps to your heart.

There will be someone who gone thru the darkest side of life similar if not the same and came thru the other end of the tunnel who will be there to share and help. Please let us know so we can ease our pains one inch at a time to make a mile of difference. We will then be helping others who are of same plight and each help carry on to the next and next. Help is like oxygen is aplenty to share only then the world will be a better place to live in or a good burial ground to die a happy death - While I thought that I was learning how to live, I have been learning how to die.

"If the Sun did not set, what would we know about light? If the blossom of the cherry did not blow in the wind, the stars would extinguish with a flash."

"That which is apparent _ends_. That which is subtle is _never-ending_."

www.ingramcontent.com/pod-product-compliance
Lightning Source LLC
Chambersburg PA
CBHW051221250726
48655CB00006B/2539